DEATH WARMED OVER

Funeral Food, Rituals,
and Customs
from Around the World

LISA ROGAK

TEN SPEED PRESS
Berkeley | Toronto

D0897422

Copyright
© 2004 by Lisa Rogak
All rights reserved. No part of
this book may be reproduced in any
form, except brief excerpts for the purpose
of review, without written permission of the
publisher.

Ten Speed Press
P.O. Box 7123
Berkeley, California 94707
www.tenspeed.com

Distributed in Australia by Simon and Schuster Australia, in Canada by
Ten Speed Press Canada, in New Zealand by Southern Publishers
Group, in South Africa by Real Books, and in the United Kingdom and
Europe by Airlift Book Company.
Cover and Interior Design by Lee Bearson

Library of Congress Cataloging-in-Publication Data
Rogak, Lisa, 1962-
Death warmed over : funeral food, rituals, and customs
from around the world / Lisa Rogak.
p. cm.
Includes index.
ISBN 1-58008-563-6
1. Cookery, International. 2. Funeral rites and ceremonies.
I. Title.
TX725.A1R637 2004
641.59—dc22
2003027662
First printing, 2004
Printed in Canada
1 2 3 4 5 6 7 8 9 10 - 07 06 05 04

Death Warmed Over

For Brendan and Sara,
because they get it.

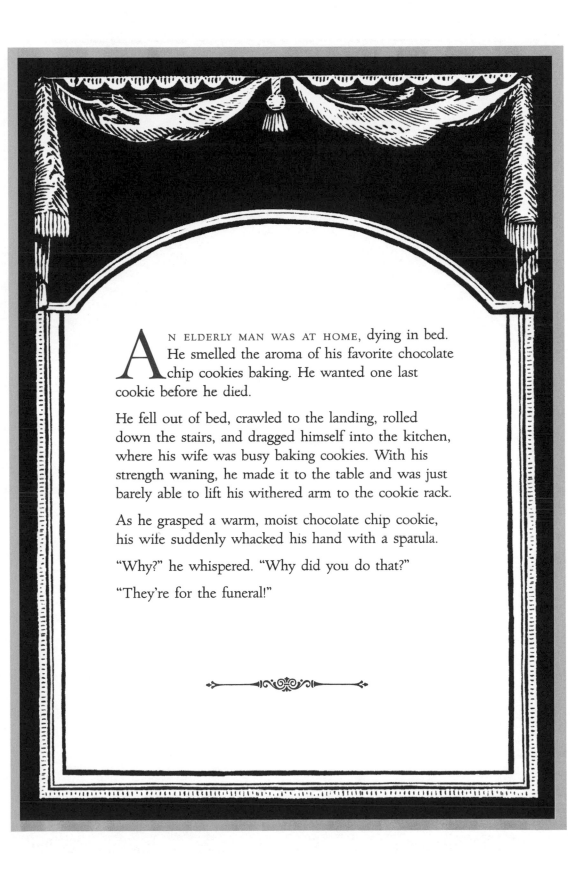

AN ELDERLY MAN WAS AT HOME, dying in bed. He smelled the aroma of his favorite chocolate chip cookies baking. He wanted one last cookie before he died.

He fell out of bed, crawled to the landing, rolled down the stairs, and dragged himself into the kitchen, where his wife was busy baking cookies. With his strength waning, he made it to the table and was just barely able to lift his withered arm to the cookie rack.

As he grasped a warm, moist chocolate chip cookie, his wife suddenly whacked his hand with a spatula.

"Why?" he whispered. "Why did you do that?"

"They're for the funeral!"

Contents

Great Britain	Morocco
Greece	Newfoundland
Greek Orthodox	New Orleans Jazz Funeral
Gypsy	Norway
Haiti	Olde England
Hawaii	Philippines
Hindu	Poland
Hmong	Protestant
Holland	Romania
Hungary	Russia
Iceland	Scotland
India	Senegal
Indonesia	Siberia (Khant)
Iran	South Africa
Ireland	Spain
Islam	Sri Lanka
Italy	Sweden
Jamaica	Switzerland
Japan	Thailand
Judaism	Tibet
Korea	Tlingit (Alaska)
Lutheran	Toraja Tribe (Indonesia)
Madagascar	Turkey
Maori	Uganda
Mexico	Vietnam
Mongolia	Zoroastrianism
Mormon	

Introduction

The History of Food and Funerals

*There is nothing like a morning funeral
for sharpening the appetite for lunch.*

—ARTHUR MARSHALL

WE IN THE WESTERN WORLD consider the concept of being a little bit dead as similar to being a little bit pregnant: it's simply not possible. Many cultures would politely disagree. For some, not only are there different degrees of dead, but they also like to keep the body around until they concur that the person is 100 percent dead, or at least 100 percent able to proceed to the next world, wherever that may happen to be. Of course, in the interim, the almost-dead still have to eat, so people in these cultures continue to serve food to their undead relative—usually foods that were favorites of the person when they were 100 percent alive. Sometimes the type and amount of food served to the formerly vibrant family member depends on how dead—or almost dead—he or she happens to be.

IT'S POSSIBLE THAT THE PRACTICE of feasting after a funeral originated with early peoples who were determined to send their dead off with some nourishment for the journey. Some cultures took this to extremes by placing a tube in the mouth of a corpse before burial, and snaking the tube out of the casket and up to ground level (once the burial was complete, of course, it would be surrounded by six feet of compacted dirt). This was to ensure that the deceased would continue to receive nourishment during the long journey into the afterlife, or at long as somebody remembered to put food down the tube. And whatever was left over, well, at least the living could eat it.

But the development of some death food customs may stem from the long journey that many mourners had to make to attend the funeral. After all, it would take a number of days for word of the demise to reach relatives living in a distant village, and then an equal number of days for them to travel to view the body and visit with the mourners. If the grieving family expected others to come, they had to be prepared to feed them.

For most cultures today, sharing a meal after the funeral has become pretty standard; indeed, it's considered rude to refuse. In any case, there's no better way to prove you're alive, in contrast to the body in the box you've just said farewell to, than by eating. (Actually, most people would claim that sex is a better way to prove this—and indeed, food combined with carnal hunger can sometimes provide a double dose of post-funeral vitality, not to mention a jump in the birth rate exactly nine months later.)

The simple truth is that food goes a long way in helping survivors cope with their loss. In *Death Warmed Over*, you'll learn how people from seventy-five different cultures and religions around the world use food in conjunction with death in ritualistic, symbolic, and even nutritious ways. Most Westerners could use a little bit of education in these matters, for when it comes to food and funerals, we in the land of milk and honey tend to be a little bit too white-bread. I mean this literally; see the Protestant entry on page 114 for an interesting way to use Wonder Bread. However, as funerals become more of a do-it-yourself proposition (not the embalming, mind you), and as more people take charge of planning their own funeral services, with a mind toward turning it into a party instead of a sobfest—thanks in part to the popularity of the TV show *Six Feet Under*—the process of learning about the funeral practices of other cultures can help us put the fun back into funeral.

SOME PEOPLE MAY BELIEVE it's distasteful to spend time thinking about how death and food are so interconnected (both are an essential part of life), but I'd like to think that many more are intrigued by discovering the differences, as well as the similarities, in how diverse cultures celebrate that connection.

When you're sharing a meal after a funeral, you're really poking a thumb in the eye of death. After all, with the simple act of eating, you're assuming that you're going to need the fuel for the future you expect you're going to have, unlike the poor body in the box whose death is the purpose for the get-together. You can ask any caterer: most people eat a lot more food at funerals than at weddings. And that cuts across all cultures.

In selecting the different cultures to profile in *Death Warmed Over*, I've chosen those that are unique or entertaining, or provide a twist to the mourning process. To that end, I've eliminated those in which the funeral customs have become overly Westernized; in some cases, I've focused on a culture whose practices may resemble ours today, but at some time in the past have been uniquely theirs.

FOR SOME OF THE CULTURES I'VE PROFILED, in which the disposition of the body is quite detailed and elaborate—and usually a 180-degree turn away from how we staid North Americans regard the corpse—I could find little information about the food and specialized dishes that are customarily served to mourners, or of distinctive culinary habits that relatives are compelled to observe. This is true of some Asian cultures, in which funeral cuisine is not specified beyond rice, vegetables, and booze, which actually could be considered the daily bread of thousands of cultures.

Since recipes for plain boiled rice and steamed local vegetables would become unnecessarily repetitive, in some cases I've taken liberties to invent dishes that reflect some aspect of mourning or treatment of the body that is peculiar to that particular group. For example, for the section on Tibetan funeral ceremonies, since the disposition of choice involves chopping up the body, mixing it with a raw savory dough, then tossing it to the vultures, I've improvised by providing a recipe for a variation on the theme of raw chocolate chip cookie dough. In place of the chocolate chips—or in place of the minced human parts—I've substituted gummy bears, or gummy humans, if you can find them. I invite you to take similar liberties if a recipe or menu I've provided just doesn't do it for you. Let your imagination go wild; as long as you incorporate some aspect of the funeral customs of a particular culture, you'll be fine. In fact, you may want to hold a potluck gathering for which you give each guest the basic lowdown on the food and funeral practices of a particular group described in this book, but not the recipe—just to see what they come up with.

One warning: Just be sure to have the number of a local Chinese take-out place handy in case things don't exactly work out. Either that, or a lot of booze. Or both. Then at least you'll be in good company with the vast majority of cultures, which take great pains to lubricate their sorrows with alcohol. And you probably won't much care how the recipes come out.

I pray that death may strike me
In the middle of a large meal.
I wish to be buried under the tablecloth
Between four large dishes.
And I desire that this short inscription
Should be engraved on my tombstone.
"HERE LIES THE FIRST POET
EVER TO DIE OF INDIGESTION."

MARC ANTOINE DÉSAUGIERS
(1772–1827)
FRENCH POET

AFRICAN AMERICAN

WHEN SLAVERY WAS STILL ESTABLISHED in nineteenth-century America, funerals were important events in the lives of the slaves, because those were truly the only taste of freedom they would experience. Not only was the ceremony often a dawn-to-dusk-to-dawn affair, but often two funerals were held for one deceased: the first shortly after the death; the second, some weeks later, when all surviving family members could travel to the grave, as well as an itinerant black preacher whose work might consist solely of traveling from funeral to funeral. In some cases, however, funerals were held only at night, to give slaves on nearby plantations a chance to sneak away for the service.

As is the case in many other cultures, slaves were often buried with their favorite foods, to sustain them for their long journey to the afterlife. According to another tradition, after the grave had been filled in and patted down, family members laid plates and utensils on top. Occasionally, broken dishes and bowls were placed on the grave to symbolize the body of a man, woman, or child who had been broken by slavery.

A chicken sacrifice was a common part of a slave funeral, not only to provide food, but also because the innards were thought to ward off bad spirits. After the meal, the surviving relatives would take the gizzards and guts into the house and set them by the chimney so that the bad spirits couldn't get in through the fireplace.

Priceless?

For composing the features	$1.00
For giving the features a look of quiet resignation	$2.00
For giving the features the appearance of Christian hope and contentment	$5.00

—FROM A FUNERAL HOME'S PRICE LIST FOR MORTUARY MAKEUP, CIRCA 1920.

Drunken Chicken

2 tablespoons unsalted
  butter
1 large yellow onion,
  minced
4 cloves garlic, minced
1 1/2 pound cooked ham,
  diced
4 chicken breast halves,
  boned and skinned
1/2 teaspoon cumin seeds
1/2 teaspoon dried sage
2 cups dry white wine
1 cup canned chicken
  stock, more if needed
1 tablespoon all-
  purpose flour
1/4 cup capers, rinsed
  and drained

Heat the butter in a small saucepan. Sauté the onion and garlic in the butter until the onion is soft.

Preheat the oven to 325°F. In a heavy 4-quart casserole, arrange half of the diced ham over the bottom. Place the chicken breasts on top, then cover with the remaining ham. Sprinkle the cumin seeds and sage over the meat mixture, and follow with the sautéed onion and garlic. Add the wine and chicken stock to cover the chicken; add more stock if necessary.

Cover the casserole with foil and bake for 25 to 30 minutes, until the chicken is done. Transfer the chicken and ham to a serving platter, reserving the liquid. In a medium saucepan, heat the liquid over high heat. Reduce it by half and stir in the flour to thicken slightly. Pour the sauce over the meat, sprinkle with the capers, and serve.

SERVES 4

AMISH

I N KEEPING WITH THE TENETS of their faith and lifestyle, Amish communities follow a path of simplicity when death takes one of their own. They and their spiritually close kin, the Mennonites, are perhaps the only people in the United States who still use a coffin—a simple, hand-built six-sided wood box—instead of a four-sided casket.

Since Amish extended families can run into hundreds of people—as a rule, they marry young and have large families—funerals are often held in the barn of the deceased. The service is held in the barn to accommodate the crowd, then the mourners eat a traditional funeral feast prepared by the female relatives and neighbors. In summertime, tables will be set outside for up to five hundred or more people, which means an immense amount of food must be prepared. But the funeral table is also simple, mostly to streamline the cooking chores for the women. Hot or cold sliced meats, cheese, vegetables, and breads are laid out on the tables.

The Death Euphemism Cookbook

Pushin' up Parsley

Peasant under Grass

Sleeping with the Quiches

Filleting the Soul

Slowly Cooling to Room Temperature

Just Add Maggots

Fettuccine Al Dead-o

Face Planting the Meringue

Still, even the local women can't prepare all the food; with families that large, funerals can be frequent, leaving little time for chores of a normal workday. Therefore, even mourners who have to travel a great distance to the funeral also contribute food to the dinner, which is how Raisin Pie—aka Funeral Pie—became a traditional dessert at Amish funerals, since it travels well.

Only after everyone has finished eating—and the women who have spent the day preparing and serving the meal have paid their respects to the deceased—does the funeral conclude with a trip to the cemetery.

Funeral Pie

1 9-inch prepared pie
crust, baked and cooled

FILLING

4 egg yolks

1 cup granulated sugar

2 tablespoons all-purpose
flour

1 teaspoon salt

2 cups milk

2 tablespoons unsalted
butter

2 teaspoons vanilla
extract

1 1/2 cups raisins

MERINGUE

3 egg whites

6 tablespoons granulated
sugar

1/4 teaspoon cream of
tartar

To make the filling, in a mixer set on medium speed or by hand, beat the egg yolks for about 2 minutes. In a separate bowl, whisk together the cup of sugar, the flour, and the salt. Slowly add the sugar and flour mixture to the yolks. Beat this mixture until it falls in ribbons from the beater blade or spoon.

Scald the milk, then add it very slowly to the egg mixture while continuously beating.

Pour the batter into a saucepan. Add the butter and cook over medium heat, stirring constantly, until the custard thickens; this will take 3 to 5 minutes. Do not let boil. Remove from the heat and stir in the vanilla and the raisins. Cover immediately with plastic wrap, being careful not to touch the surface.

Preheat the oven to 325°F.

To make the meringue, beat the egg whites to stiff peaks. Slowly beat in the 6 tablespoons sugar and the cream of tartar.

While the filling is still hot, pour it into the crust. Top immediately with the meringue and spread to the edges. Bake for 20 to 25 minutes, until browned. Cool on a rack. Serve warm or at room temperature.

SERVES 10

BALINESE PEOPLE WHO TODAY regard themselves as thoroughly modern tend to incorporate their mixed heritage into their funeral ceremonies, which include rituals from Indonesia and Java, as well as Polynesia and China.

It's among Bali's primitive tribes that the traditions involving funerals and food get interesting. After death, a kind of Chinese water torture is performed on the body; it is laid on a table, and a stream of water slowly drips onto the body. Just below this setup, the family places a cradle filled with unhusked rice so that as the water runs off the body it drips directly onto the rice, along with any liquid leaching out of the body. None of my sources reveal how long the rice is steeped in this corpse water, but afterward the body is buried and the rice is shaken from the husks, then cooked as usual. Before serving, the rice is shaped into the form of a human, and then all the tribe members eat it.

In another Balinese tribe, the corpse is set on a wooden platform near a cliff. In most cases, wild animals and birds will make quick work of the remains after three days; this is referred to as "air burial." If the creatures were less than diligent, the tribe interprets this to mean that the spirits don't want the body. If it's not good enough for the spirits, the tribe doesn't want it either—they then shove the body off the cliff, nearer to the critters' lairs, in hopes that they'll take the hint.

Some Things Never Change

According to two University of Pennsylvania archaeologists who were conducting research at the 2,700-year-old tomb of King Midas in Turkey in 1999, the mourners at the king's funeral feast ate a lamb and lentil stew. They also drank heartily, a mixture of wine and beer that the ancient Greeks called *kykeon*. The researchers tested trace residues on the bowls and drinking utensils found in the tomb for their findings, and they planned to hold a re-creation of the feast the following year.

Balinese Black Rice Pudding

To create a human shape, use a 3- to 4-cup copper mold in the shape of a gingerbread man.

½ cup black glutinous rice (available from Asian markets)
⅓ cup white glutinous rice
3 ¼ cups water
¼ cup granulated sugar
1 8-ounce can coconut cream

Mix the black and white rice in a colander and rinse under running water to remove the starch. Place the rice and 3 cups of the water in a heavy saucepan over high heat. Bring to a boil, then lower the heat and simmer, stirring occasionally, for about 30 minutes.

In a small saucepan, add the sugar to the remaining ¼ cup of water. Slowly add the coconut cream. Bring to a boil and simmer for about 5 minutes, until a syrup forms. Set aside.

When the rice has simmered for about 30 minutes, add the sugar syrup and continue to simmer gently until most of the liquid has evaporated. The rice should now be a dark purple color.

Lightly grease the copper mold. Transfer the rice into the mold and even out the top with a knife. Cool and serve.

SERVES 4

BELGIUM

THROUGHOUT THE CENTURIES, Belgium has been invaded by almost every other European country. It's only natural to ask *Why?* The beer? The chocolate? The waffles? I suppose each of the invaders had their own reasons, but, happily, since medieval times the Belgians have been able to exact their revenge when it came to food: they just borrowed a little bit from each of the occupying forces, then combined them to create a new cuisine all their own, with the best from France, Spain, Russia, and the other infidels who have tried to overtake this genteel country.

When it comes to funeral food in Belgium, it seems that black is the key. In fact, color is frowned upon, so as better to reflect the starkness of death. That's why slices of crisp black bread—known as *simnel cake* and often referred to as "soul bread'"—and chocolate *anything* tend to be the foods of choice before, during, and after a funeral. Chocolate cake with dark chocolate frosting served on black plates is, of course, ideal. Red wine is forbidden due to its color, so white wine is served instead. Maybe this custom attempts to achieve some kind of Zen balance to the *black = death, white = life* formula. Anyway, with that in mind, most Belgians wouldn't frown on you if you were to opt for a vanilla glaze on the Belgian Funeral Cake instead of the chocolate glaze described here.

Pig in a Poke

A Chinese friend once told me that he had offered a pig to the dead [as an offering]. "A whole pig?" I asked, somewhat surprised, since I knew he was far from being a rich man. He laughed. "No, we fool them. What we do is offer the head and the tail, maybe the feet. Then they fill in the blanks and assume we gave the rest, too."

—NIGEL BARLEY

Belgian Funeral Cake

CAKE

2 1/3 cups granulated
  sugar

1 2/3 cups unsweetened
  cocoa

2 1/4 cups water

2/3 cup vegetable oil

3 large eggs

2 tablespoons sour cream

2 teaspoon vanilla
  extract

2 1/4 cups all-purpose
  flour

3 tablespoons cornstarch

2 1/2 teaspoons baking
  soda

1/2 teaspoon salt

GLAZE

1/2 cup heavy cream

8 ounces semisweet choco-
  late, chopped

Preheat the oven to 325°F. Grease two 9-inch round cake pans.

To make the cake batter, sift the sugar and cocoa together into a large bowl. Whisk in the water, followed by the oil, eggs, sour cream, and vanilla. In a separate bowl, stir the flour, cornstarch, baking soda, and salt together. Whisk the dry mixture into the wet mixture and stir until smooth. Pour into the pans and bake 40 to 45 minutes, until a cake tester comes out clean. Cool in the pans on racks for 10 minutes. Carefully remove the cakes from the pans; cool completely.

To make the glaze, heat the cream in a small saucepan over high heat until it boils. Remove from the heat and add the chocolate. Stir until smooth. Turn one of the cakes upside down and spread it with half of the glaze. Place the other cake on top, right-side up, and pour the rest of the glaze over the top.

SERVES 10

BRAZIL

PEOPLE IN SÃO PAULO and the other major Brazilian cities tend to follow Western traditions when it comes to funerals. As is the case in Bali, it's the tribal people living in the jungles and mountains who still incorporate food into their mourning rituals in unusual ways.

When a member of the Kaingang tribe dies, the others believe that the "ghost soul" of the deceased will stick around the village for a while, in order to select a helpmate from among the survivors. A ghost soul is a clear threat to the survivors, since this means that one of them must die—usually the widow or widower. The tribe casts the surviving spouse out of the camp, then puts them through a purification ritual so that the ghost soul will fail to recognize their spouse. The ghost soul will wander away from the tribe in despair, never to return. At that point, the spouse can return to the tribe.

These purification rituals of course involve food. While living outside the village, the spouse is forbidden to eat any cooked food, but must subsist on raw vegetables and honey. The spouse is supposed to hunt and kill an animal while cast out from the village, but is forbidden to eat it; instead, the outcast slits open the animal and smears the blood onto his or her body, in order to confuse the ghost soul.

The closest you'll probably come to duplicating this experience is by eating raw vegetables with a honey-based dip. This dip needs to be refrigerated a couple of hours for the hot and sweet flavors to integrate, so be sure to allow time for this.

More Death Euphemisms

Gone to cultivate chile peppers

Taking an early bath

Eating dandelions by the roots

Hearing the final whistle

Stretching out your legs

Gone up into the woods

Crudités with Honey Mustard Dip

¼ cup spicy brown
   mustard
1 tablespoon mild
   yellow mustard
1 tablespoon white
   vinegar
Dash of onion salt
Dash of red pepper
   flakes
1 ½ cups mayonnaise
¼ cup light corn syrup
¼ cup honey
¼ cup peanut oil
Assorted raw vegetables,
   such as carrots,
   celery, red and green
   bell peppers,
   cucumber, broccoli,
   and cauliflower, cut
   up for dipping

In a medium-sized bowl, combine the two mustards and the vinegar, onion salt, and red pepper flakes. Add the mayonnaise, corn syrup, honey, and peanut oil to the mustard mixture and whisk until smooth. Refrigerate for at least two hours before serving.

MAKES 3 CUPS OF DIP

BRITTANY

RITTANY, A REGION OF NORTHWESTERN FRANCE, is a veritable hotbed
of funeral food superstitions and rituals, probably due to its Celtic heritage. The Breton people believe that when a person dies from cancer,
it's imperative to set a dish of butter on a nearby table so that the cancer will penetrate the butter. The survivors then take the dish outside and bury
it to ensure that no other family members contract the disease.

Milk can stay in the room, but water can't, since it's believed that the soul,
newly freed and unaccustomed to wandering, can easily fall in and drown in
the water.

Even the dead, who are supposedly resting in peace at the graveyard, aren't
excused from these superstitions. An old Breton custom dictates that the dead
have to eat as much dirt in death as the amount of bread that they wasted in
life. And their duties don't end there. The society of people long dead and
buried even has special rules for newcomers. In a Breton graveyard, the person
buried most recently in the
cemetery serves as a watchman
over the graveyard until the next
newly dead person comes to
relieve him of his duties. But it's
not an entirely thankless task,
for the cemetery sexton or
gravedigger will usually leave a
box of tobacco and a pipe for
the newest watchman, so that
those hours of mindless tedium
contain at least a little pleasure.

It's Not the Humidity, It's the Heat

A company called ExtremeFood.com offers
Blair's Death Sauce, Original Death Sauce,
Sudden Death Sauce, and 3 A.M. Reserve,
which clocks in at anywhere from 1,500,000
to 2,000,000 Scoville units. (According to the
site, "In 1912 Wilbur Scoville developed a
test to measure the heat of a pepper. Bell
peppers range from 0 to 100 Scoville units,
while pure capsaicin ranks about 15,000,000.
The habañero pepper tests out about 200,000
to 300,000 scovilles.") The company's motto
is Feel Alive!

Brittany Funeral Fish Soup

3 pounds mixed white-
  flesh fish (such as
  flounder, mackerel,
  cod, haddock), boned
  and cleaned

3 tablespoons unsalted
  butter

2 large yellow onions,
  thinly sliced

3 cloves garlic, crushed

6 russet potatoes, peeled
  and quartered

10 cups water

1 bay leaf

1 teaspoon thyme

1 teaspoon marjoram

4 sprigs parsley

1 teaspoon salt

1 teaspoon freshly
  ground black pepper

8 thick slices crusty
  French bread

Cut the fish into bite-sized chunks. In a large Dutch oven or stockpot, melt the butter. Sauté the onions and garlic until the onions are translucent. Add the potatoes, water, bay leaf, thyme, marjoram, parsley, salt, and pepper. Bring to a boil over high heat. Add the fish. Decrease the heat to medium. Cover and cook for about 25 minutes, until the fish and potatoes are tender. Remove the bay leaf. Ladle soup into deep bowls and serve with the bread.

SERVES 6 TO 8

BUDDHISM HAS MILLIONS OF FOLLOWERS in almost every country in the world. Like Christians, when it comes to funerals and death rituals, Buddhists take the basic tenets of their religion and usually add a few of their own cultural and geographical influences.

Food plays a vital role in the Buddhist funeral ceremony. One surefire way to get in good with the Buddha is to give food to the monks during the pre- and post-funeral services. It is thought that by doing so, a Buddhist can increase his chances for attaining nirvana, though at the time of a relative's death he has the option of giving that good will to the deceased, since the dead are obviously closer to nirvana than the living.

Cremation is common for Buddhists, but in countries where wood is scarce, ground burial, air burial, and even water burial are practiced instead. Buddhist temples typically allow some personalization of the ceremony, but in addition to an open casket, it's standard practice for an altar to be placed near the casket with a bowl of water and incense, flowers, fruit, and a candle arranged on top.

Sometimes, a pair of chopsticks used by the deceased is set standing up in a bowl of uncooked rice on the altar during the funeral, but more often this is used on the Buddhist altar at the home of the deceased, with the rice used as an offering to Buddha. There-

There's a Tear in my Beer

According to the Code of Hammurabi of ancient Babylonia, a merchant could be put to death for diluting beer.

fore, you may want to keep the position of your chopsticks in mind the next time you eat at an Asian restaurant. In the same vein, it is very much frowned upon to use chopsticks to pass food from one person to another at the table. This act resembles a Buddhist funeral rite in which, after cremation, the bone fragments of the deceased are passed from one relative to another using chopsticks. To make sure you don't commit any faux pas during a Buddhist post-funeral gathering, it's a good idea to stick to dishes that don't require the use of chopsticks. Miso soup is one of them.

Miso Soup

6 cups water

6 tablespoons white
   miso paste

3/4 pound fresh peas,
   shelled

3 green onions, with the
   tops, thinly sliced

1 jalapeño pepper,
   seeded and thinly
   sliced

1 clove garlic, minced

1 teaspoon lemon juice

1/2 teaspoon hot sesame
   oil

Place 1 **cup** of the water and the miso in a small bowl and stir together. In a large pot, mix together the remaining 5 cups of water and the peas, green onions, jalapeño pepper, and garlic. Cover and bring to a boil over medium-high heat. Decrease the heat and simmer for three minutes. Stir in the miso mixture along with the lemon juice and hot sesame oil. Bring to a simmer over medium-high heat. Serve immediately.

SERVES 6

I F YOU HAPPEN UPON A CAJUN FUNERAL, you may get the impression that you've arrived at a party instead. That's what it is. In fact, this festive post-funeral mood is only one of several customs Cajuns share with Mexicans. Another is the annual November 2 celebration known as *le Jour des Morts*, or the Day of the Dead, when families visit the cemeteries where their loved ones and ancestors are buried, decorate with flowers, place food on the graves, and generally have *les bon temps*.

In the days before telephones, people used to drape a quilt over the railing of the front porch to announce to neighbors any kind of news in the family: a birth, an engagement, or a death. And one Cajun superstition says if you found an alligator under your house, death was imminent.

But What a Way to Go

In the St. Giles section of London on October 17, 1814, a tank at a London brewery exploded, releasing 3,500 barrels' worth of beer. The beer flooded homes and businesses in the vicinity, crushing two homes and drowning nine people in the wave of suds.

In the old days, when funerals were conducted at home in the front parlor, the feet of the deceased were always pointed toward the door, to facilitate his journey into the next world. It's a widespread custom among many other cultures for those in the house where a death has occurred to open the windows to allow the soul to escape; in Cajun country, when someone had died, during the procession from the house to the cemetery the neighbors would always keep their doors and windows shut so that the spirit wouldn't wander in by accident. But in another way, Cajun culture was like many others: as the news of a neighbor's death spread, women set to preparing food to bring to the family.

Cajun Funeral Cake

The pecans and pineapple make this a true Cajun cake.

CAKE

2 cups all-purpose flour

2 teaspoons baking soda

2 eggs

2 cups sugar

1 12-ounce can crushed pineapple with juice

ICING

1 cup sugar

1 6-ounce can evaporated milk

1 cup pecans, chopped

½ cup (1 stick) margarine

Preheat the oven to 375°F. Grease and flour a 9 by 13-inch glass baking dish.

To make the cake, in a large mixing bowl, combine the flour with the baking soda. While constantly stirring, add the eggs, the sugar, and the pineapple with its liquid. Mix until well combined. Pour into the baking dish. Bake for 30 minutes, or until a knife inserted comes out clean. Cool completely on a rack before icing.

While the cake is baking, make the icing. Mix the sugar, evaporated milk, pecans, and margarine together in a medium saucepan. Bring to a boil. Decrease the heat and cook, stirring occasionally, for 10 minutes, or until slightly thickened. Let cool. Cool the icing completely before spreading onto the cake.

SERVES 12

Among the ancient celts, the festival of Samhain was held for seven days each autumn to remember the death of the Sun God and prepare for his travel to Tir-fo-Thonn—the land under the sea—where he could assume his rightful place as Lord of the Death.

In Celtic homes, funeral rituals were patterned after some of the Samhain rites. First, a wake was held in the deceased's home for seven days and nights. The body was washed, preferably with seawater, since that would protect it during the trip to Tir-fo-Thonn. It was then wrapped in a special death shirt called an *eslene* and set on a platform or casket bier in the exact center of the house. Villagers would come by the house and participate in a kind of chant-ing called *caoine* (a term that evolved into the word *keening*), in which wails are interspersed with praise and memories of the deceased. This *caoine* stage lasted about three days. After that, the mourners and family took stock of how well they'd keened over the corpse, and if all were satisfied, they moved on to the party stage, complete with feasts and games.

At that point, mourners turned downright jovial. It was customary to place gold and weapons on the bier alongside the casket, and also to set a bowl of food on the chest of the corpse during the dancing and singing. This stage lasted four more days, until the burial.

Colcannon, a traditional Celtic dish, is the perfect meal to set in a bowl and place on the chest of a corpse during a wake . . . or to enjoy by yourself while sitting upright and alive.

Colcannon

6 large russet potatoes,
   peeled and cut into
   1-inch chunks
3 tablespoons vegetable
   oil
3 cloves garlic, minced
1 head cabbage, thinly
   sliced
1 large leek, white part
   only, trimmed and
   thinly sliced
½ cup (1 stick)
   unsalted butter
Salt and freshly ground
   black pepper

Place the potatoes in a large stockpot, cover with water, and boil until tender. Drain.

While the potatoes are cooking, heat the oil in a large frying pan. Add the garlic and sauté until golden. Add the cabbage and leek and cook until tender. Set aside.

Mash the butter into the warm potatoes and add salt and pepper to taste. Add the cabbage and leek mixture to the potatoes and stir well.

SERVES 6

CHINA

Though the "official" Chinese state religion is an amalgam of Buddhist, Tao, and Confucian beliefs, with a pinch of Shamanism thrown in for good measure, the truth is that the primary religion in China is ancestor worship. This, combined with food, plays an important part in any Chinese funeral ceremony.

During the wake, the family schedules a number of receptions for mourners to attend. The deceased is placed in a coffin, which is set near the tables at the reception area. Incense burns on top of the coffin all day and all night, and when anyone is eating in the vicinity, a plate of food is set near the coffin.

On the day of the funeral, the family gathers to eat breakfast, a dish of *jai*, also known as Monk's Food. You may have seen it on the menu at Chinese restaurants, where it's often called Buddha's Delight. Though *jai* is a dish that's traditionally served during the Chinese New Year, it's also eaten before a funeral, since death is considered to be a new beginning for the deceased. Once guests start to arrive for the ceremony, they are given a coin and a piece of candy to sweeten their sorrow. In remote areas of the country, relatives will sacrifice a cow to satisfy the gods and the ancestors in the hopes that they won't need to take another human, via death, in the near future.

Three days after the burial, relatives and friends come to the cemetery to set food, flowers, and candy beside the fresh grave. Then, for a full year after the date of death, a stone tablet inscribed with the name of the deceased has a place of honor in the home. The family places a bowl of rice, meat, and vegetables before the tablet twice a day, in the morning and evening.

Buddha's Delight (*Jai*)

¼ cup black tree-ear fungus

¼ cup dried snow fungus

½ cup dried bean-curd stick

½ cup dried bamboo piths

½ cup long rice

1 cup peanut oil

8 ounces tofu, cut in 1-inch cubes

4 cups shredded bok choy

½ cup sliced carrots

½ cup bamboo shoots

3 tablespoons soy sauce

1 tablespoon sugar

3 cups water

½ cup black mushrooms, soaked in warm water for 15 minutes, drained, and dried

½ cup straw mushrooms

½ cup raw peanuts

1 teaspoon sesame oil

Salt

In separate small bowls of warm water, soak the black tree-ear fungus, snow fungus, bean-curd stick, bamboo piths, and long rice for 15 minutes, then rinse and drain.

In a wok, heat the peanut oil over medium-high heat until sizzling. Deep-fry the tofu for 5 minutes, or until golden. Transfer the tofu onto paper towels to drain. Pour off and discard all but ¼ cup of the oil. Reheat the remaining oil in the wok over medium heat. Add the bok choy, carrots, and bamboo shoots; stir-fry for 1 minute.

Add the black tree-ear fungus, snow fungus, bean curd stick, bamboo piths, long rice, fried tofu, soy sauce, and sugar, stirring constantly.

Add the 3 cups of water, black mushrooms, straw mushrooms, and peanuts. Bring to a boil. Decrease the heat to low, cover, and simmer 20 minutes, or until the vegetables are tender. Season with the sesame oil and salt to taste.

SERVES 6

WHEN AMERICA WAS STILL a British colony, funeral customs
tended toward the rituals that were followed in the colonists'
homelands. After all, in the eighteenth century most colonists
had not been born in the new country; even if they had, how-
ever, their parents and grandparents still followed traditions from their old land.

Among German settlers in Pennsylvania, when a relative died, the family sent
a rider out on horseback to friends and relatives with an invitation to the funeral,
a bottle of wine, black gloves, and a pair of *doed-koecks* (dead cakes). Seems like a
nice way to invite people to a funeral, even today.

Other colonists had a peculiar custom involving a bottle of Madeira: the cask
would first be opened at the wedding of a local man, then sealed tight and not
reopened until the time came for the man's funeral. Some fans of really good
Madeira may have thought twice about toasting a long life to the happy couple.

Among other Pennsylvania colonists, when the mother of the house died, it was
the custom to shake up a bottle of vinegar and to turn barrels and crocks of wine,
pickles, and fruit stored in the cellar upside down in the belief that the presence
of death in the house would cause the sediment in these foodstuffs to spoil. Then,
after the funeral and burial, the villagers laid out such a feast that one wag observed
that the occasion seemed less like a funeral and more like Thanksgiving Day. And
in some communities, the women were forbidden from walking in a funeral procession from a home or church to the cemetery, so the men left—while the women
stayed behind at the deceased's home and ate cookies and drank Madeira.

Although the early colonists didn't have cans of cream of chicken soup and
cornflake crumbs sitting on their shelves, they did often make a casserole of
Funeral Potatoes to bring to a household where a death had occurred. After all,
potatoes were cheap and available—and could be stored for months in the root
cellar—and it took little time to stir together a casserole for a grieving neighbor.

Funeral Potatoes

6 cups peeled, diced
    russet potatoes
1 10¾-ounce can
    condensed cream of
    chicken soup
½ soup-can whole milk
1 cup sour cream
1 cup grated sharp
    cheddar cheese
¼ cup grated onion
Salt and freshly ground
    black pepper
4 tablespoons (½ stick)
    unsalted butter
1 cup cornflake crumbs

Place the potatoes in a large stockpot with enough water to cover. Salt lightly. Bring to a boil and cook for 10–15 minutes, or until there's still a bit of bite to the potatoes. Drain the potatoes and arrange them in a greased 3-quart casserole dish.

Preheat the oven to 350°F. In a medium bowl, combine the soup, milk, sour cream, cheese, and onion. Add salt and pepper to taste. Pour over the potatoes.

In a small saucepan, melt the butter over a low flame. Remove from the heat. Add the cornflake crumbs and stir until mixed and crumbly. Sprinkle over the casserole. Bake uncovered for 30 to 45 minutes, until the crumbs are lightly browned and the potatoes are bubbling.

SERVES 8

ALTHOUGH THERE ARE MANY HOLIDAYS throughout the year when a home cook in the Deep South can show off her culinary talents, it seems to be a funeral that makes her pull out all the stops, so that a funeral feast can quickly resemble a bake-off at the county fair. Of course, fried chicken would be first on the list, followed by massive jugs of sweet tea and 1950s-era cake carriers filed with coconut cake, pecan pie, and the ubiquitous Jell-O salad molds. While the post-funeral meal could take place in a restaurant or at a relative's home on the dining room table, more often than not they are held in the kitchens and function rooms of the church of the deceased.

As Michael Lee West writes in her marvelous book of food-obsessed essays, *Consuming Passions,* there are rules to be followed when preparing funeral food.

"This is not the time to bring *Better than Sex Cake* or *Death by Chocolate,*" she writes. "Another improper funeral dish is baked beans . . . unless you lay in a supply of Beano, this condition is not welcome in closed-up houses and funeral parlors."

Eat Cake

The now-defunct Jones Mortuary, in Greenville, South Carolina, used to provide a chocolate cake to each family they served. It was baked by the mother of the owner, and delivered to the residence where the family was gathering.

For those not food-inclined, West wisely suggests that a package of paper plates, plastic eating utensils, or a pound of coffee will always come in handy. In any case, the food brought to a Deep South funeral—or indeed, to any funeral—should always convey the feeling that you're sorry for the family's loss and that bringing food is one way you can help.

Southern Fried Chicken

3 cups all-purpose
flour
1 tablespoon seasoned
salt
1 tablespoon garlic
powder
1 tablespoon onion
powder
1 teaspoon coarsely
ground black pepper
2 eggs
4 cups buttermilk
1 cup barbecue sauce
2 tablespoons
Worcestershire sauce
1 tablespoon steak
sauce
2 cups oil for frying
1 whole frying chicken,
cut into pieces

In a large shallow dish, mix together the flour, seasoned salt, garlic powder, onion powder, and pepper. In a separate bowl, beat the eggs, then whisk in the buttermilk, barbecue sauce, Worcestershire sauce, and steak sauce.

Heat the oil in a large, deep skillet to 375°F. Dredge the chicken first in the liquid mixture, then in the seasoned flour, dipping alternately in each at least twice.

Cook the chicken in the hot oil for about 15 minutes on each side, until golden brown on both sides.

SERVES 4

THROUGHOUT THE SMALL rural towns of Denmark, it's still possible to find cabinetmaker's shops that offer residents a sideline in caskets. Although this was the custom in many countries—including the United States—in towns large and small well into the early twentieth century, today the combination cabinet/casket shop is pretty much extinct.

But not in the Danish countryside. Until recently, the funeral industry in Denmark was nonexistent, and family members with a loved one to bury assumed most of the responsibilities themselves. As recently as the early 1960s, embalming was rare and funerary cosmetics unknown, and funeral directors did not have what we know as a funeral home, only a storefront to display caskets and urns.

As you might expect, the treatment of the body is pretty simplified as well: it is dressed in either pajamas or a simple shirt. And instead of resting in a padded satin casket liner, the body is tucked in between bedsheets.

The gathering of mourners after the funeral and the food served also follow the same rule of simplicity. The group either gathers at a local restaurant for coffee or congregates back at the home of the family for a smorgasbord of whatever happens to be on hand, combined with whatever people have brought to share.

Have It Your Way

The website for the Texas Department of Criminal Justice lists the last-meal requests of prisoners about to be executed. There are lots of requests for shrimp, cheeseburgers, and french fries, although a couple of unusual items may make you wonder about the crimes that landed the prisoners there in the first place. Three of the standouts are Cool Whip and cherries; one bag of assorted Jolly Ranchers; and one cup of hot tea (from tea bags) and six chocolate chip cookies. The website claims that "The final meal requested may not reflect the actual final meal served."

Funeral Smorgasbord

8 large romaine lettuce leaves

6 eggs, hard-boiled and quartered

12 small cooked shrimp, peeled
  and deveined

1/4 pound smoked salmon

1/4 pound smoked herring

1/4 pound whitefish, thinly sliced

1/2 pound Virginia ham, sliced

1/2 pound roast beef, sliced

1/4 pound Danish blue cheese,
  cubed

1/4 pound Danish hard cheese,
  cubed

3 medium tomatoes, cut into
  wedges

3 navel oranges, peeled and
  sectioned

1 red onion, sliced

3 medium Granny Smith apples,
  cored, cut into wedges, and
  dipped in lemon juice

1 Vidalia onion, sliced

24 pimiento-stuffed green olives

1 12-ounce jar dill pickle slices

1/2 cup mayonnaise

1/2 cup mild yellow mustard

1/2 cup cocktail sauce

1 loaf rye bread, thinly sliced

1 5-ounce package crispbread

Line 2 large platters with 4 lettuce leaves each. On each platter, arrange the egg, shrimp, fish, meats and cheeses, and fruits and vegetables. Spoon the condiments into small bowls and place near the trays. Arrange the bread slices in baskets and serve buffet-style.

SERVES 12

ECUADOR

THIS SMALL SOUTH AMERICAN COUNTRY, stretching from the Pacific Coast over the Andes Mountains to the Amazon drainage, has a population of mixed Spanish and native Indian ancestry. Though the funeral customs in a major city like Quito are relatively westernized, in the mountainous regions of the country the funeral customs could be described as colorful.

While the body is laid out, mourners place items for the afterlife around it, including food, drink, and utensils. Some also place a couple of sprigs of rosemary next to the body, as Ecuadorians consider this herb to be a lethal weapon in the next life. One of the mourners cuts a lock of hair from the body and burns it. The resulting ashes are mixed with some of the food served at the funeral feast, and all guests are expected to partake of it.

Later, after the burial, the family wraps a meal consisting of cooked potatoes and corn in a cloth and sets it on top of the just-covered grave. Though the family refers to it as a "lunch for the dead," everyone understands that this is part of the payment the gravediggers receive for doing their job.

Then there's the Jivaro tribe, who were once notorious headhunters (the practice is now illegal). Their modus operandi in battle was to kill their enemies and bring the heads back home, where they would first boil them, then lay them out in the sun for weeks or months to thoroughly dry them out. Once they were the proper size to thread on a necklace, they were done. The necklaces were brought out mainly to display at various festivals held during the year.

When the owner of the shrunken-head necklaces died, however, the trophies were not handed down to the younger generation, but instead were typically buried with the owner, probably to the great dismay of the other Jivaros.

A glass of good wine is a gracious creature, and reconciles poor mortality to itself, and that is what few things can do.

—SIR WALTER SCOTT

Potato and Corn Cakes

2 pounds russet pota-
toes, peeled and sliced

4 tablespoons (¹/₂ stick)
butter

2 medium onions,
finely chopped

3 cups corn kernels,
fresh or canned

1 cup peanut oil for
frying

In a large stockpot, place the potatoes in enough salted water to cover. Bring to a boil and cook until soft. Drain and mash until smooth.

Heat the butter in a large saucepan and sauté the onions until translucent. Add the onions to the mashed potatoes, mixing well. Stir the corn into the potato-onion mixture. Shape the potatoes into 12 balls, then flatten to form cakes about 1 inch thick.

Pour the peanut oil into a large saucepan, adding more if necessary to cover the bottom of the pan. Heat over medium-high flame for a minute. Place the potato cakes in the oil and cook, flipping once, until they are golden brown on both sides, approximately 7 to 10 minutes on each side.

SERVES 6

EGYPT

TODAY, EGYPTIAN CULTURE is primarily Muslim, and funeral customs in the country generally follow traditional Islamic principles, including the distribution of food to the local poor. But aside from today's Islamic rituals, Egyptian funeral food has a long and illustrious past. In fact, it's possible that the first time you learned that food was connected with funerals was in history class when you got to the chapter about the Egyptians and the pyramids. Archaeologists working inside the pyramids have uncovered evidence of elaborate feasts that lasted for days, but this custom was not reserved for Egyptian royalty; the common Egyptian also received a funerary feast send-off into the next world. In fact, the earliest known records of Egyptian funerals show proof of food offerings to the dead, both to the newly deceased and to the family's ancestors. It seems that the living always went all out, as if to ensure a place for the deceased as well as to get in good with the gods upstairs for when their own time would come.

Comestibles, from beer and wine to cakes and even the intact head of a bull, were used as funeral offerings in ancient Egypt. This makes sense when you consider that in those days each man was expected to devote one-fifth or more of the value of his estate to the cost of his funeral, which required feeding all the guests—both the living relatives and the dead ancestors.

CAKE

1 ³/₄ cups unbleached flour

2 teaspoons baking powder

1 teaspoon cinnamon

1 teaspoon ground cloves

¹/₂ cup brewed coffee

4 ounces (4 squares) semisweet baker's chocolate

¹/₂ cup (1 stick) unsalted butter

1 cup sugar

2 eggs

1 teaspoon vanilla extract

¹/₂ cup milk

CINNAMON WHIPPED CREAM

2 cups whipping cream

2 teaspoons vanilla extract

¹/₄ cup sugar

¹/₂ teaspoon cinnamon

Ancient Egyptian Chocolate Cake

To make the cake, in a medium-sized bowl, sift together the flour, baking powder, cinnamon, and cloves. Set aside.

In a small saucepan over low heat, stir the coffee and chocolate together until the chocolate is melted. Set aside.

Preheat the oven to 350°F. Grease and flour two 8-inch round cake pans. Using an electric mixer on low speed, cream the butter and sugar in a mixing bowl until fluffy. Add the eggs, one at a time, beating until smooth. Add the vanilla and the coffee-chocolate mixture, beating until smooth. Add the flour mixture and the milk alternately, beating until smooth after each addition.

Pour the batter into the pans. Bake for 30 minutes, or until a tester comes out clean. Cool in the pans on a rack for 15 minutes. Invert the pans and cool the cakes completely on the rack.

To make the cinnamon whipped cream, while the cake is baking and cooling, chill a mixing bowl and beaters. Combine the whipping cream, vanilla, sugar, and cinnamon and whip until thick enough to spread.

To assemble the cake, place one cake layer upside down on a serving plate and spread with whipped cream. Place the second cake layer on top, right side up. Frost the sides and top with the remaining whipped cream. Refrigerate until ready to serve.

SERVES 10

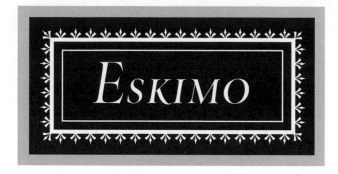

ESKIMO

W HERE I LIVE, IN RURAL NEW HAMPSHIRE, the old-timers will some-
times tell stories about how hard the winters were in the Good
Old Days. It soon turns into a variation on *Your Mama Is So Fat:*
"Why, they were so rough," a geezer will start jawing, "that one
January we had to put Grandma out in a snowdrift
because we didn't have enough food to go around."

Then the next one will start in. "Oh *yeah*? Well,
I remember one winter we were snowed in so bad
that when Uncle Charlie died, we had to keep him
in the basement until the roads opened in May!"

As with most tall tales, there is a grain of truth
to these stories, and they bear some resemblance
to the stories about how the Eskimo dealt with
relatives who were on their deathbed. For them,
however, it had nothing to do with waiting until
the spring thaw. Instead, the Eskimo used to bring
dying family members to special huts on the
periphery of the village. The huts were made from
blocks of ice; inside the hut, the relative would
soon die. The rationale was that this would prevent the ghost of the deceased from haunting the
living. Ghosts weren't too smart, the thinking
went, so if they started to wander off, the only
place they'd be able to find again was the site of
their death—or, from the ghosts' point of view, the
site of their birth.

I'm not sure about the current situation, but in
ancient Eskimo days there were two food groups:
blubber, and everything else. For a funeral feast,
they may have gone all out, opting for bearded
seal as opposed to everyday seal.

You Want Fries with That Casket?

Put one of the most popular
uses of the Web to use for
you. Everybody eats, and
most everybody cooks. If you
like to cook, post some of
your favorite recipes online.
Be sure to add new ones
each month to give commu-
nity residents a better flavor
for your family.

If you're not such a creative
cook, ask the community to
email recipes to you for various dishes you'd like to try,
and post these recipes on
your website. Not only will
this generate a lot of visits to
your site, you'll never have to
buy a cookbook again.

*—from "Ten Great Ideas for
your Funeral Home Website"
Courtesy Aurora Casket
Company (auroracasket.com)*

Savory Oogruk (Bearded Seal) Flippers

To prepare these properly takes at least two weeks, so be sure to plan ahead.

*Flippers from
  1 oogruk
Fresh blubber,
  as needed*

Remove the flippers from the oogruk. Place the flippers in a vat of fresh blubber. Set aside to marinate.

After two weeks, take the flippers out of the vat of blubber. Strip the fur from the flippers. Cut the flippers into chunks and serve.

SERVES 4

ANY EASTERN EUROPEAN CULTURES have innumerable superstitions about daily life and nearly as many about death, although many of these beliefs clearly contradict one another. Estonia is no exception. A person in one Estonian village might think that it's a good sign if someone eats right before death, since a person who dies with an empty stomach may come back to haunt his family for food while they sleep. However, someone the next village over may believe that if a person on his deathbed eats something just before death arrived, his family will encounter hardship and hunger in the days to come. According to yet another superstition, if the family ignores a relative's last request, regardless of whether he asked to be fed or not, they will increase their chances of being haunted by that relative's ghost in the future.

It just goes to show you that you can't win. As is the case with medical studies—you can always find one to support the unhealthy habit you just can't give up, especially when it comes to food—in Estonia it's easy to find a superstition to support a particular food custom.

The funeral feast for the survivors begins when the last shovelful of dirt hits the coffin. The mourning family arranges for pastries, bread, wine, and vodka to be served to those attending the funeral, which is held at the graveside. Some cemeteries even have large shelters on the premises, designed to shield mourners from bad weather.

Whatever food and drink is left over after the mourners have had their fill is usually left in the cemetery; to bring it home would only invite more death into the house. Later that same day, another funeral feast is served by the villagers back at the home of the deceased. This meal is more substantial, with several courses served, including roast pork, chicken soup, macaroni, and cabbage rolls.

Estonian Cabbage Rolls

1 head cabbage

1 1/2 pounds lean ground
beef

1 large onion, chopped

1 cup cooked rice,
(1/2 cup uncooked)

1 medium egg

1 teaspoon salt

1/2 teaspoon freshly
ground black pepper

1 tablespoon paprika

1 16-ounce can sauer-
kraut, drained

1 16-ounce can tomato
sauce

Core the cabbage head and place it in a large bowl. Add boiling water to cover and let stand five minutes. Drain the cabbage well and remove the leaves, cutting off the thick ends of the stems. Set aside.

Preheat the oven to 350°F. In a medium-sized bowl, combine the meat, onion, rice, egg, salt, pepper, and paprika. Take a cabbage leaf and put two tablespoons of filling in the middle. Fold the leaf over the filling like an envelope. Place seam side down in a 13 by 9-inch baking pan. Repeat until all the leaves and filling are used up.

Spread sauerkraut on top of the rolls. Pour the tomato sauce on top of that. Cover with foil and bake for 40 minutes, or until the meat is cooked through.

SERVES 8

I N MANY CULTURES, bringing food to the home of a family who has just lost a relative is a way to say that you care and you wanted to do something. In Ethiopia, however, women who go to the house of a mourning family are *required* to bring either food or coffee or they're not allowed to enter the home. Men, on the other hand, can visit empty-handed. They usually bring booze for the mourning family; however, they are not required to show up with a bottle until the second visit. This custom resulted, in part, out of necessity. An Ethiopian family is not allowed to prepare any food in the house of mourning, so relatives and other villagers pitch in. During that week, the family not only eats other people's food, but they must also sleep on the floor and wear the same clothes at night that they wore all day long.

> In Brittany, where honey formed an important part of the midnight repast in the death chamber, a curious superstition existed. A little fly was thought to appear on the lips of the corpse, from whence it would presently go to the jar of honey, from which it would take its fill. The fly was none other than the soul of the departed, fortifying itself before taking its long journey into the distant spirit-world.
> —BERTRAM S. PUCKLE

When the official mourning period ends, after about a week, most of the household routines return to normal, although widows and widowers can continue to mourn for a year or more without repercussion from relatives or villagers. Some let personal grooming fly totally out the window: men may go a year without shaving, and women will tie their hair back with rags and do nothing to it for months.

In fact, the official sign that the mourning period is over is when the widow rubs butter into her hair. Occasionally, when the villagers and relatives think she's mourned long enough, they will take matters into their own hands and slather butter on her hair themselves.

Spiced Butter *(Niter Kebbeh)*

2 pounds (8 sticks)
  unsalted butter, cut
  into small pieces
1 onion, coarsely
  chopped
3 tablespoons minced
  garlic
2 tablespoons minced
  fresh ginger
1 teaspoon ground
  turmeric
1 teaspoon ground
  cardamom
1 cinnamon stick
1 whole clove
1/4 teaspoon ground
  nutmeg
Injera (Ethiopian
  flatbread) or other
  flatbread

In a large saucepan, melt the butter slowly over medium-low heat. When it is completely melted, increase the heat to high and add the onion, garlic, ginger, turmeric, cardamom, cinnamon, clove, and nutmeg. Stir to blend. Decrease the heat to low and simmer uncovered for 45 minutes. Do not stir. The milk solids on the bottom of the pan should be golden brown, and the butter on top should be clear.

Slowly pour the clear liquid into a bowl, straining through cheesecloth. It is important that no solids are left in the niter kebbeh. Transfer the liquid into a jar. Cover tightly and store in the refrigerator for up to one week. Serve spread on flatbread.

MAKES 2 CUPS

ETRUSCAN

THE LAND OF THE ANCIENT ETRUSCANS was centered around the city of Caere, Italy, in what we know today as the Tuscany region, north of Rome. Wealthy Etruscan families of the time—the fifth century B.C.—followed the patterns of Egyptian royalty: they liked to have painters create panoramic scenes on the insides of their tombs, which were similar to our mausoleums today. The tomb was intended to be a nice enough home for the dead that their spirits wouldn't begin to roam and haunt the living.

The Etruscans believed that once a body was interred inside the tomb and the stone was rolled into place to seal off the burial space, the souls of the dead came alive: they basically partied and feasted all day and night. The key to encouraging the dead to remember to do this, however, was to have scenes painted on the tomb walls picturing banquet tables laden with plenty of roast meats, ripe fruit, and pitchers filled with wine. In fact, the painters hired by the families were essentially recreating the image of a typical Etruscan funeral feast. Etruscans believed that having paintings of food and drink on the tomb walls was the only way to ensure that the dead would have enough to eat.

After the feast scene was completed by the painter, the surviving family members would place a table and chairs inside the tomb. They would roll back the stone for regular visits and bring actual food and wine to place on the table, both for the deceased and to serve as offerings to the gods. Occasionally, the family would sacrifice a chicken inside the tomb, being careful to allow the earth to absorb all of the blood from the bird. The Etruscans thought that in addition to the food and wine—real and painted—in the tomb, the dead also required a regular dose of blood from an animal sacrifice or they would really die and totally cease to exist.

Grapes and bread were standard fare for the fashionable Etruscan tomb. Here's a recipe that combines both.

Etruscan Grape-filled Bread

*1/3 cup extra-virgin
olive oil, plus more
for topping*

1 sprig fresh rosemary

*1 1-ounce package dry
yeast*

*1 cup lukewarm water
(90° to 100°F)*

*4 cups all-purpose
flour, sifted*

*1/2 cup plus 2 table-
spoons sugar*

*2 pounds green seedless
grapes, stemmed*

In a small saucepan over a low flame, heat the oil and rosemary for 5 minutes. Remove from the heat and allow to cool. In a small bowl, dissolve the yeast in the water. Set aside.

Put the flour in a large mixing bowl. Pour the yeast mixture into the center and stir to incorporate. Remove the rosemary from the oil. Add the oil to the dough along with 2 tablespoons of sugar and mix until just combined. Turn out onto a floured board and knead until smooth, about 10 minutes. Place in a large greased bowl, cover with plastic wrap, and place in a warm area for about an hour, until doubled in size. Punch down the dough and divide it in half.

Preheat the oven to 350°F. Grease a 13 by 9-inch baking pan. On a floured board, roll out half of the dough to fit in the pan. Cover with half of the grapes, sprinkle with 1/4 cup of the remaining sugar, and drizzle with 1/3 cup olive oil. Roll out the other half of the dough to fit. Seal together the top edge of the dough with the bottom layer. Lightly push down on the dough to crush the grapes. Cover the top layer of dough with the rest of the grapes, sprinkle with the remaining 1/4 cup sugar, and drizzle with olive oil. Place a cookie sheet on top of the grapes and press down to crush them. The dough will absorb the juice. Bake until golden, about 40 minutes.

What will be the death of me are bouillabaisses, food spiced with pimiento, shellfish, and a load of exquisite rubbish which I eat in disproportionate quantities. —EMILE ZOLA

A FRENCH FUNERAL IS A SIGHT to behold. Even though modernity has taken over much of the country—especially in the customs of the younger generation—French funeral rituals are still a monument to tradition and the old-time French way of doing things. This is most obvious in the French casket, which is a simple wooden six-sided coffin in the shape of a small boat. For an adult, a black cloth is draped over the coffin and a plaque with the initials of the deceased is set on top of the cloth. For a child, a white cloth is used. Whether the wake is held at home or in a funeral home, candlelight is still preferred to electric illumination. Most often, a form of standing candelabra known as a *herce* (harrow) is used to hold the candles. This word is the origin of the English word *hearse*.

Until 1904, the Catholic Church assumed exclusive responsibility for administering all funerals across the country, but today local governmental officials work in tandem with either the church or the funeral home to ensure that everything runs smoothly.

Turkey Day

Duggan's Serra Mortuary in Daly City, California, which conducts over a thousand funerals each year, presents each family with a cooked turkey at the cemetery, at the conclusion of the graveside service.

The following recipe, Chicken in Half-Mourning, also known as Black and White Chicken, provides food and alcohol in one dish, which means it is more than appropriate to serve at a post-funeral feast.

Chicken in Half-Mourning

You'll need cheesecloth and kitchen string to assemble the dish.

1 4-pound broiler chicken, whole, rinsed and patted dry

1 black truffle, very thinly sliced

8 cups chicken stock (canned is fine)

4 large carrots, peeled and sliced

6 leeks, washed, green parts removed

With your fingers or a butter knife, gently loosen the skin over the breast and thighs of the chicken, being careful not to tear the skin. Insert the truffle slices under the skin along each breast and over each thigh.

Wrap the chicken in the cheesecloth, smoothing it over the bird. Secure the loose fabric with kitchen string.

Pour the chicken stock into a large Dutch oven. Add the chicken, carrots, and leeks.

Place over a high flame and cover. Bring to a boil, then lower the heat and simmer gently for 45 minutes. Remove from the heat and set aside, still covered.

After a half hour, lift out the chicken and remove the cheesecloth. Place the chicken on a serving platter and arrange the carrots and leeks around the chicken.

SERVES 4

ALTHOUGH GERMANS GENERALLY have a reputation of being extremely detail-oriented and very determined to carry out tradition in their own fashion, they are notably more relaxed in their funeral customs. For one thing, the funeral service is typically held not before the trip to the graveyard, but right in the cemetery at the graveside. The grave is usually dug in the hour or two before the time of the service; then the minister proceeds with the service, which in the middle of winter will be understandably abbreviated.

> Wish I had time for just one more bowl of chili.
> LAST WORDS OF KIT CARSON

After the minister flings some dirt on top of the casket, the mourners follow his lead; then the gravediggers finish their job. Depending upon the weather, the mourners may choose to plant flowers on the slightly raised mound immediately after the service concludes, or wait until another day, or season.

As is the case with the majority of cemeteries in European countries, once the casket is buried this does not necessarily mean that the body will spend eternity in the same spot. Most German cemeteries operate on a leasing system: a family can lease a grave for anywhere from twenty-five years to sixty years or more, and subsequent generations can renew the lease for additional periods. If the lease is not renewed, the body and headstone are removed and the remains are reburied elsewhere in the cemetery, in a communal mausoleum known as a *knochenhaus*.

It's somewhat surprising that Germans accept this impermanence of their loved ones' resting place so nonchalantly, but it is common custom—and after losing a high percentage of historic buildings and sites during bombing raids in World War II, the Germans know about impermanence. For example, Saint John Cathedral in Leipzig, the site of J. S. Bach's burial, was destroyed in an air raid in 1943; after the war ended, his remains were moved to another cathedral.

Red Cabbage

½ pound bacon, diced

4 pounds red cabbage, cored and shredded

1 large yellow onion, diced

1 head garlic, peeled and minced

1 quart beef stock

1 bottle dry red wine

½ teaspoon nutmeg

1 teaspoon cinnamon

Salt and freshly ground black pepper

1 cup brown sugar

1 cup red wine vinegar

In a large, heavy stockpot, fry the bacon until browned. Don't drain off the fat. Instead, add the cabbage, onion, and garlic to the pan. Cook over medium heat until the cabbage begins to wilt.

Add the stock and the wine to the cabbage. Continue to cook until the cabbage softens and the liquid is reduced by half. Add the nutmeg and cinnamon and season with salt and pepper to taste. Mix in the sugar and vinegar; adjust the quantities to taste. Continue to cook until most of the liquid is evaporated, about 20 minutes.

SERVES 10

F OOD AND DRINK FUNERAL CUSTOMS in Ghana are all about liquid: water, wine, and rum. All play an important role in helping the spirit of the dead move on. Among the Ashanti tribe of Ghana, when a person is dying, a group of watchers consisting of medicine men and witch doctors incessantly stare at the dying to watch for the exact moment of death. When they determine that it has arrived, they pour a trickle of water into the just-deceased's throat. This is to ensure that the spirit is able to climb up the precipitous hill that will guide him in the direction of eternity without becoming thirsty. So important is this rite of passage that the watchers believe if they miss the moment of death by more than a few seconds, they themselves will be struck down early and fail to live to a ripe old age.

After the water, the watchers pour rum down the throat of the deceased. They position the body so that it is lying on its left side, so the deceased can use the right arm and hand for eating. As payment for these tasks, the watchers are paid with bottles of wine.

The mourning period can then begin; it lasts two days and two nights. During this time, the immediate family is required to fast, although they can drink red wine. The deceased, on the other hand, is allowed to eat, or at least provisions are placed by the body to be taken on the journey. Typically, a chicken, eggs, and a bowl of mashed sweet potatoes are prepared for the dead, along with a jug of water.

On the third day after death, the corpse is buried in the tribal burial ground. The family—still fasting—and mourners drink more red wine and pour some on the grave. The family spends the fourth day after the death thanking relatives and villagers for helping, but still they fast. Finally, on the fifth day, the family is allowed to break the fast, usually with a freshly killed sheep.

Ghanaian Lamb Stew

3 pounds boneless lamb
  shoulder
1 cup water
1 teaspoon nutmeg
1 green bell pepper,
  seeded, deribbed,
  and chopped
2 teaspoons minced
  fresh ginger
2 cloves garlic, minced
2 medium tomatoes,
  peeled and chopped
1 tablespoon fresh
  lemon juice
1 teaspoon salt
1 teaspoon freshly
  ground black pepper
1 bay leaf

In a large stockpot, place the lamb, water, nutmeg, green pepper, ginger, garlic, and tomatoes. Cover and cook over medium heat for 30 minutes. Add the lemon juice, salt, pepper, and bay leaf and continue cooking slowly until the liquid is almost gone and the meat is tender.

SERVES 10

GREAT BRITAIN

FUNERAL SERVICES IN GREAT BRITAIN still, for the most part, convey the stiff-upper-lip attitude we Yanks have associated with Brits ever since we tried to make tea in Boston Harbor. Not much has changed in the U.K. since those days when it comes to either tea or death. Since tea is such a part of daily life in Great Britain, it's no surprise that a common English custom is to hold a "Funeral Tea" at a nearby restaurant or at the home of one of the mourners or relatives right after the service.

Another old English custom involved placing a cup of wine directly on the coffin. Mourners stood in a circle around the coffin and took turns drinking from the cup, a kind of communion service with the dead person.

Of course, in Britain a good part of the appeal of any tea is the food that goes along with it. Ham has been a traditional component of any Funeral Tea for so long that it is typical for mourners to ask if the deceased is "being buried with ham." Whether supplied by a caterer or prepared and brought by friends or relatives to the supper after the trip to the cemetery, ham is a perfect funeral food: it will keep for several days, can be eaten at any meal, and is a sweet and salty comfort food that takes a tiny bit of the sting out of the traditional British funeral, thus helping them keep that stiff upper lip firmly in place until later.

About a century ago, when raising livestock was common in Britain, most families raised a pig for food. The family couldn't kill their own pig, but had to trade pigs with a neighbor or another family member in order not to kill their own. This goes right along with the stiff-upper-lip custom of the Brits; killing a pig that belongs to someone else helps keep the emotions at bay.

A Culinary Epitaph, Take One

HERE LIES THE BODY OF OUR ANNA
DONE TO DEATH BY A BANANA
IT WASN'T THE FRUIT THAT LAID HER LOW
BUT THE SKIN OF THE THING THAT MADE
HER GO.

Buried with Ham

The ham must marinate for at least two days, so be sure to plan ahead.

1 7-pound pork picnic shoulder, bone in

2 cups brown sugar

1 teaspoon whole cloves

1 cup honey

1 6-ounce can frozen orange juice concentrate, thawed

Place the ham in a large, deep bowl and add enough water to cover it. Add the sugar and stir. Cover with foil and marinate at least 2 days in the refrigerator.

Preheat the oven to 200°F. Completely line a roasting pan with heavy-duty foil. Drain the ham and set it in the pan. Stick the cloves into the ham in a uniform pattern. Mix together the honey and the orange juice concentrate and pour it all over the ham.

Cover tightly with foil. Bake for 6 to 7 hours, or until done. Every hour, unwrap the ham and baste it with the honey mixture. When the ham is done, increase the heat to 450°F, uncover the ham, and bake for another 15 minutes or so to crisp the exterior.

SERVES 12

GREECE

SOMETIMES IT SEEMS LIKE the most important part of a Greek funeral is knowing who to bribe. The primary aim of Greek culture is to please the gods—any and all gods—at weddings, births, and funerals. Before leaving wine and water at the side of a freshly dug grave to assist the deceased on their journey, mourners had to appease the gods. Of course, significantly more wine than water was left at the gravesite, since in ancient Greece, wine was a lot safer to drink than water.

Sour Milk

When a person died in seventeenth-century Scotland, the surviving family members were required to throw away all of the milk, onions, and butter that were in the house at the time of death. The belief was that the soul of the deceased would defile these foods in some way.

Then, at the funeral feast, before digging in, they had to thank Demeter for the bread and Dionysus for the wine and any lamb, beef, or pork dishes on the table.

The priests had to be bribed as well, not only immediately after the funeral, but also on specific days after the death, in order to help the priests remember to pray for the soul of the deceased. The mourning family typically presented the holy men with a bowl of cooked corn mixed with sugar. The corn represented the resurrection of the soul; the sugar stood for a blissful future in heaven.

Mourners were served a similar dish called *kolliva*, but this was made with cracked wheat instead of corn. Some Greeks believed that the only way to ensure that the gods would forgive the sins of the deceased was for the surviving relatives and friends to eat plenty at the funeral.

Two other funeral customs of the ancient Greeks are worth noting. First, it was customary to set a jug of water on the grave of a dead man who had never married, drawing attention to the fact that he had never participated in the washing ritual that many Greeks undertake before the wedding. Second, many people believed that the soul could not leave the body of a dead person unless all the rings were removed from the hands.

Kolliva

1 cup wheat berries

4 quarts water

1 cup raisins

1 cup chopped walnuts

½ cup honey

1 teaspoon cinnamon

¼ cup confectioners'
    sugar

⅓ cup Jordan almonds

In a large stockpot, stir the wheat berries into the water. Bring to a boil, decrease the heat, and simmer over a low flame, stirring occasionally, for about 2 hours, until tender.

Drain the wheat in a colander and spread it out onto a large towel for about a minute to absorb the remaining water.

Put the wheat in a large mixing bowl and add the raisins, walnuts, honey, and cinnamon. Mix well. Let cool.

When cool, pour the mixture out onto a large serving platter and shape into a mound. Sift the sugar over the top, covering evenly.

Use the Jordan almonds to form a cross on top of the mound. Serve immediately.

SERVES 8

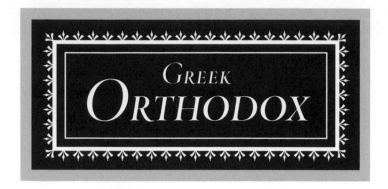

GREEK
ORTHODOX

A T SOME GREEK ORTHODOX burial services this old custom is still followed: at the gravesite, the priest reads a passage from the Bible while the mourners munch on what amounts to trail mix. The Bible passage? "The earth that fed you now shall eat you."

Gets right to the point, doesn't it? The Greek Orthodox religion is nothing if not direct, and it doesn't stray far from that straightforwardness when it comes to telling its followers how to view the afterlife. In their eyes, the next world is just a different form of purgatory. It is believed that upon death a person gets the low-down on the difference between heaven and hell, and what can be expected from each. Then the soul of the deceased sits and waits.

It'll be a looooong wait. According to the Greek Orthodox Church, the final fate of a soul is not determined until Judgment Day, so colorfully described in the book of Revelations.

Fortunately, those left behind don't have to wait that long for the post-funeral meal. Tradition dictates that a "mercy meal"—most often served at a nearby restaurant—be offered to mourners. A mercy meal is also served at the Greek Orthodox Easter; it consists of baked fish.

At the funeral, mourners are expected to kiss the Orthodox cross on the body in the open casket. Mourners are supposed to wear blue or black, preferably formal clothing. After the funeral, a memorial service is held at the church on the Sunday closest to the fortieth day after death; this service is often followed by another mercy meal that again features baked fish.

The Bee's Knees

Upon the death of a family member, an old English custom was to find the nearest beehive and tell the bees about the death. Neglecting this step was thought to cause the bees to abandon the hive, creating a dearth of future honey stores for the survivors. In fact, many churches kept beehives to ensure a steady supply of wax for funeral candles; beeswax is the dark yellow color the Catholic church required for its masses for the dead. In fact, it was not unusual for a parishioner to will his hives to the church upon death, which was one way to make sure the priest put in a good word for the deceased.

Mercy Meal Fish

1 red snapper, 2 1/2 to
    3 pounds, cleaned, with
    head and tail left on
1 teaspoon salt
Juice of 1 lemon
1 tablespoon dried
    oregano
Freshly ground black
    pepper
1/2 cup + 1 tablespoon
    olive oil
1 large yellow onion,
    chopped
1/4 cup chopped parsley
2 cloves garlic, minced
1 pound new red potatoes,
    sliced
6 medium tomatoes,
    peeled and sliced
1/2 cup fresh bread
    crumbs
1 lemon, thinly sliced
1 bay leaf

Sprinkle the fish with the salt. Score the fish by making three diagonal cuts about 1 inch apart and 1/2 inch deep. In a small bowl, combine the lemon juice, oregano, and black pepper. Press the mixture into the cuts on the fish.

Grease a 13 by 9-inch baking dish with 1 tablespoon of the oil. Place the fish in the dish, and brush another tablespoon of oil over the fish. Cover and set aside.

Heat 1/4 cup of the oil in a heavy skillet over medium heat. Add the onions and sauté for 5 minutes. Stir in the parsley and garlic and remove from the heat.

Preheat the oven to 350°F. Spread the onion mixture over the fish, along with the potatoes and tomatoes. Drizzle the remaining 1/4 cup oil on top. Sprinkle the bread crumbs on top and arrange the lemon slices and bay leaf on the fish. Bake for 30 minutes, or until the fish feels firm.

SERVES 4

A T A TYPICAL GYPSY FUNERAL, whether held in the United States or abroad, more than one onlooker has been prompted to ask, "What's the party for?" When a Gypsy dies, it's not uncommon for others to travel across the country for the funeral. State laws dictate that a body must be embalmed if the service will be held several days after the death; after the funeral director performs this task, the Gypsies take over, from welcoming guests during the wake to cleaning up afterward and, most important, making sure that the body is never alone.

A table is kept stocked with food and replenished during the wake, which lasts all day and night, usually for three days, with the open casket not far away. A favorite food on the menu is fish, but other meats and foods are in ample supply throughout the wake. Once the funeral party arrives at the cemetery, mourners set food and drink onto the casket as it is lowered, and they spill wine into the grave as it is filled in. Some Gypsy tribes spread a tablecloth on the ground next to the just-covered grave and have a picnic of cold meats and cheeses; others wait until they return to the home of the deceased.

Superstitions about Death

Through the ages, people have used food and signs that they read into it—the lack or abundance thereof, or the way it's positioned, or cooked, or whatever—as indications of an impending death. Here are a few food superstitions:

- If a person who's ill suddenly asks for a mug of hard cider, it's a sign he's going to die.

- If fruit and flowers appear on a tree simultaneously, death will come to the house nearby.

- When making a food offering to the dead, the food should always be placed at the burial site, or else the soul will wander back to the house where he spent his previous life and haunt the people still living there.

- If thirteen people sit down at a table to eat, one of them will die before the year is over.

Gypsy Potatoes

¹/₂ cup olive oil

*2 pounds red bliss or
other red-skinned
potatoes, peeled and
sliced*

*2 tablespoons caraway
seeds*

*4 tablespoons (¹/₂ stick)
unsalted butter , at
room temperature*

*Salt and freshly
ground black pepper*

Preheat the oven to 400°F. Pour the oil into a roasting pan and heat in the oven for 10 minutes.

Remove the pan from the oven. Spread the potatoes over the bottom of the pan. Return to the oven and roast, uncovered, for one hour, until the potatoes are crisp on the outside and tender inside. A few times during the baking, shake the pan to toss the potatoes so they brown evenly.

Add the caraway seeds and butter and mix well to melt the butter and coat the potatoes with the seeds. Season with salt and pepper to taste.

SERVES 8

HAITI

I N HAITI, EVEN THOUGH THE OFFICIAL national religion is Catholicism, the art of voodoo rules all passages in life, from birth to marriage to death. In voodoo, death is thought to be not the end of life, but a stage of transition from one bodily form to another. The *corps cadavre* (body) is merely the vessel for the two main parts of the soul, known as the *gros bon ange* (large good angel) and the *ti bon ange* (small good angel). The large angel represents the person's life force or energy, the small angel the person's personality.

A Culinary Epitaph, Take Two

HERE LIES JOHNNY COLE,

WHO DIED, ON MY SOUL,

AFTER EATING A PLENTIFUL DINNER;

WHILE CHEWING HIS CRUST,

HE WAS TURNED INTO DUST,

WITH HIS CRIMES UNDIGESTED,
  POOR SINNER.

The purpose of a Haitian death ritual is to ensure that both angels are sent to their proper places: the large angel is sent to Ginen, a place where the spirits of all Haitian ancestors reside, while the small angel first floats around the body for nine days after death, then is banished to the grave by capturing it in a jar and then burning it. If the large angel does not reach Ginen, Haitians believe that the spirit will haunt the surviving relatives. If the small angel is not successfully trapped in the grave, it will haunt not only relatives, but also strangers all around the world. Understandably, Haitians take extra effort to ensure that each angel travels to its proper home.

Each voodoo ritual is an intricate, intensive art, which leaves little time for the daily routines of life, like preparing meals. The recipe included here is a popular dish that requires little tending or maintenance—the perfect meal for busy voodoo practitioners on the go.

Griots

2 pounds boneless pork
  shoulder, cubed

1 Spanish onion,
  chopped

1/4 cup chopped fresh
  chives

1/2 cup freshly squeezed
  lime juice

3 1/4 cups water

Pinch of dried thyme

1/4 teaspoon salt

1/4 teaspoon freshly
  ground black pepper

1 1/2 cups uncooked
  white rice

3 tablespoons peanut oil

Place the pork, onion, chives, lime juice, 1/4 cup of the water, thyme, salt, and pepper in a large bowl and stir to coat. Cover and place in the refrigerator to marinate for a few hours. Drain the pork, reserving the marinade.

In a medium saucepan, cook the rice with the remaining 3 cups water while you prepare the meat. In a large skillet, heat the oil over medium heat. Add the pork and stir until browned, about 5 minutes. Add the marinade, cover, and simmer over low heat for 30 minutes. Serve hot over rice.

SERVES 6

OFF-ISLANDERS MAY CONSIDER POI to be the standard Hawaiian dish, but the truth is that today, the food served at traditional Hawaiian funerals most often resembles the dishes served at more upbeat Hawaiian events like a luau. It seems that almost every funeral custom practiced in old Hawaii—that is, before the twentieth century—involved some sort of symbolic tradition. In the early 1800s, when Queen Kamamalu's husband died, she had a tattoo put on her tongue. An Englishman, the Reverend William Ellis, observed the procedure, and later he commented to her that it looked incredibly painful. The queen responded, "The pain is indeed great, but the pain of my grief is greater."

Historians and archaeologists have discovered that in old Hawaii the deceased body was customarily wrapped in banana, taro, and mulberry leaves before being buried near the structure that served as the community dining room for male villagers.

> **Cookbooks We're Glad We Never Used**
>
> *The Little Cyanide Cookbook: Delicious Recipes Rich in Vitamin B17,* by June DeSpain
>
> (The recommended book that Amazon.com pairs with DeSpain's cookbook is unfortunately entitled *Alive & Well.*)

Roast pig served on banana leaves was the customary funeral food, with an elaborate carving ceremony conducted by the chief of the village. Plenty of kava— a nonalcoholic but euphoria-inducing drink made from crushed herbal roots—was served on the side. One expert on Hawaiian customs advises those of us living in modern times that "a carton of corned beef may be substituted for a pig."

A *lau lau* is a popular item at Hawaiian funeral feasts. It is a serving of spicy pork, chicken, fish, or vegetables wrapped in taro leaves, then cooked in a steamer or pressure cooker.

Lau Lau

18 large ti leaves
(available at
Hawaiian groceries)
18 luau (taro) leaves
(available at
Hawaiian groceries)
6 boneless chicken
thighs
1 pound boneless pork
shoulder, cut into
6 portions
1 pound salmon, cut
into 6 portions
4 1/2 teaspoons salt

Wash the ti and luau leaves and remove the stems and fibrous parts of the veins.

Set the luau leaves on a flat surface; place one piece of meat (chicken, pork, or salmon) on each leaf. Sprinkle each piece of meat with 1/4 teaspoon salt. Wrap the leaf around the meat to form a bundle. Place the bundle on the tip end of a ti leaf and wrap tightly; fasten with toothpicks or tie with kitchen string. Assemble the remaining bundles in the same manner.

In 3 separate steamers, bring water to a boil. Place all the *lau lau* in the steamers; lower the heat and simmer for 4 to 6 hours, until done replenishing the water as necessary.

MAKES 18 LAU LAU

HINDU

URING THE FIRST twenty-four hours after death, cooking within the household of the deceased is prohibited, and though relatives and friends can bring food to the house, close family members usually fast on the first day.

Cremation, the normal mode of disposing of bodies for Hindus, is customarily done a day or two after death. However, to ensure the secure passage of the soul to the next world, a ceremony known as a *shraddha* must be performed. The *shraddha* is an elaborate feast and gift-giving event; Hindus believe that everything that is given away will eventually end up in the hands and stomach of the deceased. Some *shraddhas* last one day; others can go on for weeks. Feasts can be elaborate, or they may merely consist of rice and vegetables, along with the chapati (round flatbread) that's served at most Hindu meals.

To successfully complete each *shraddha,* however, the *manes*—the spirits of other dead relatives—must be appeased. Because they're used to being dead, they're easily gratified with boiled rice balls called *pinda,* which are thrown out the door after each meal. Those still alive, however, require something a little bit more substantial, like samosas.

2 cups all-purpose flour

2 teaspoons salt

½ cup plus ½ teaspoon peanut oil

7 tablespoons water

4 unpeeled russet potatoes, boiled and allow to cool

1 medium onion, minced

1 cup fresh shelled peas

1 tablespoon finely grated fresh ginger

1 hot green chile, finely chopped

3 tablespoons finely chopped fresh cilantro

1 teaspoon ground coriander seeds

1 teaspoon garam masala

1 teaspoon cumin

½ teaspoon cayenne pepper

2 tablespoons freshly squeezed lemon juice

Peanut oil for deep frying

Samosas

Sift the flour and ¹/₂ teaspoon salt into a large bowl. Add ¹/₄ cup of the oil and mix into the flour until the mixture resembles coarse breadcrumbs. Slowly add 4 tablespoons of the water and mix until you can gather the dough into a stiff ball; sprinkle with more water if necessary.

Transfer the dough onto a floured board. Knead the dough for about 10 minutes, or until smooth. Make a ball. Rub the ball with ¹/₂ teaspoon of the oil and slip it into a plastic bag. Set aside.

Peel the potatoes and cut them into ¹/₄ inch dice. In a large saucepan, heat the remaining ¹/₄ cup of oil over a medium flame for a minute. Add the onion. Sauté until translucent. Add the peas, ginger, green chile, cilantro, and the remaining 3 tablespoons of water. Cover, decrease the heat, and simmer until the peas are cooked, about 10 minutes. Add more water if necessary.

Uncover and add the potatoes, the remaining 1¹/₂ teaspoons salt, coriander, garam masala, cumin, cayenne, and lemon juice. Stir to mix. Cook on low heat for 3 to 4 minutes, stirring gently. Remove from the heat and let cool.

Turn the dough out onto a floured board and divide into eight balls. As you work with each, keep the rest covered. Roll the ball out into a 7-inch round. Cut in half with a sharp knife. Take one half and form a cone, with a ¹/₄-inch overlapping seam. Secure the seam with a dab of water. Fill the cone with 2¹/₂ tablespoons of the potato mixture. Pinch the top of the cone closed by creating a ¹/₄-inch seam, secured with a dab of water. Using the prongs of a fork, seal the top seam. Proceed with the rest of the dough and filling until you have 16 samosas. Cover.

In a large saucepan or wok, heat 2 inches of oil over a medium-low flame. When the oil is heated, gently place a few samosas into the oil, or as many as the pan will hold in a single layer. Fry the samosas, turning frequently, until they are golden brown and crisp, 8 to 10 minutes. Drain on paper towels and serve.

MAKES 16 SAMOSAS

A HMONG FUNERAL is considered to be the most important event in a person's life, since doing it right ensures that the deceased will flourish in the next life. Do it wrong and, well, let's just say it won't be as much fun. Once deceased, a Hmong begins a very long journey, and the surviving friends and relatives make sure to prepare him well for the trip with sufficient food, wine, money, and clothing, along with specific directions to the land of his ancestors through traditional funeral songs and chants.

Most Hmong funerals last for three days before the burial. Because the rooster symbolizes vitality to Hmong people, a rooster is often sacrificed to escort the soul of the deceased on his trip. In addition, each child of the deceased parent provides a cow to be sacrificed, to provide food for the funeral feast.

Essentially, a funeral for an elder Hmong is viewed as repayment by their children for the sacrifices the parents made for them. As a result, some Hmong funeral feasts feed hundreds of people for several days.

The Hmong will perform a ceremony on the first anniversary of the death to invite the soul back for a final feast. Another cow is usually sacrificed at this service, to ensure that the soul makes its final ascent to its ancestors.

EGG ROLLS

One 10 1/2-ounce packa[ge]
  bean thread noodles
1 small head green
  cabbage, shredded
2 carrots, shredded
1 yellow onion, minced
1 bunch green onions,
  minced
1/2 bunch cilantro, min[ced]
1 1/2 pounds ground por[k]
1 egg
2 teaspoons freshly
  ground black pepper
2 teaspoons salt
2 tablespoons oyster
  sauce
2 tablespoons fish sauc[e]
2 tablespoons soy sauce
1 package rice paper
  sheets
1 egg beaten with
  1 tablespoon water
Peanut oil for deep-fry[ing]

Hmong Egg Rolls

RED PEPPER DIPPING SAUCE

5 Thai red chile peppers

1 clove garlic, minced

1 tablespoon chopped
   green onion

1 tablespoon chopped
   fresh cilantro

1 teaspoon freshly
   squeezed lime juice

1/4 cup fish sauce

2 tablespoons water

In a medium bowl, cover the bean thread noodles with boiling water. Let stand for 10 minutes.

In a large bowl, mix the cabbage, carrots, onion, green onions, cilantro, ground pork, and egg. Stir thoroughly. Add the black pepper, salt, oyster sauce, fish sauce, and soy sauce and mix until combined.

Drain the noodles and roughly chop them into 3-inch lengths. Add to the cabbage-pork mixture and stir well.

Peel one sheet of rice paper at a time from the package. Place 1/4 cup of the noodle-pork mixture on the sheet. Roll up and fold like an envelope. Secure the seams with a dab of the beaten egg and water. Repeat with the rest of the sheets until the noodle-pork mixture is gone.

Heat 2 inches of oil in a wok or large heavy skillet. Gently place the egg rolls into the oil and cook for about 10 minutes.

While the egg rolls are cooking, prepare the dipping sauce. In a small bowl, combine the red peppers, garlic, green onion, cilantro, lime juice, fish sauce, and water, and mix well.

Serve hot egg rolls with dipping sauce.

MAKES 24 EGG ROLLS

Everyday cookies in Holland were called iron cookies, named after the wafer irons used to make them—little flower shapes at the end of a long steel rod with a handle. Today, you can often see them in use at country fairs in Pennsylvania Dutch country.

The Dutch reserved a more serious type of cookie for funerals. Called funeral cakes, they are a kind of thick round cookie made from a mixture of flour, sugar, eggs, and caraway seeds. Like the funeral biscuits served at Olde English funerals, the Dutch funeral cakes were often handed out to mourners as they left the service. However, instead of printing the name of the deceased on the outside of the wrapper for these take-out cookies, as the old-time Brits did, the Dutch had the initials of the dead person imprinted directly on the funeral cakes themselves. Whether they were carved or spelled out with caraway seeds is uncertain, but, like the English, many mourners didn't eat them but held onto them for years, sometimes decades, as a reminder of the dead.

Rest in Piece

Veteran Pillsbury spokesman Pop N. Fresh died yesterday of a severe yeast infection. He was 71.

Fresh was buried in one of the largest funeral ceremonies in recent years. Dozens of celebrities turned out, including Mrs. Butterworth, the California Raisins, Hungry Jack, Betty Crocker, and the Hostess Twinkies.

The graveside was piled with flours as longtime friend Aunt Jemima delivered the eulogy, describing Fresh as a man who "never knew how much he was kneaded." Fresh rose quickly in show business, but his later life was filled with many turnovers.

He was not considered a very smart cookie, wasting much of his dough on half-baked schemes. Still, even as a crusty old man, he was a roll model for millions.

Fresh is survived by his second wife; they have two children and one in the oven. The funeral was held at 3:25 for 20 minutes.

Funeral Cakes

1 ½ cups granulated
  sugar

1 ½ cups all-purpose
  flour

1 tablespoon baking
  powder

2 large eggs, beaten

1 cup milk

¼ cup (½ stick)
  unsalted butter,
  melted and cooled

1 teaspoon vanilla
  extract

¼ cup confectioners'
  sugar

½ cup chocolate
  sprinkles

Preheat the oven to 400°F. Grease and flour 18 cups of standard-size muffin tins, or use paper muffin cups.

In a mixing bowl, combine the sugar, flour, and baking powder. Set aside. In a small bowl, combine the eggs, milk, melted butter, and vanilla. Add the liquid ingredients to the flour mixture and stir until just blended.

Fill the muffin cups halfway. Bake for 12 to 15 minutes, until a tester comes out clean.

Let cool on racks for 15 minutes. Sift a light layer of confectioners' sugar over each cake, then decorate with chocolate sprinkles, spelling out the initials of the deceased.

MAKES 18 CAKES

DESPITE HUNGARY'S REPUTATION as a country that's more modern and Western than others in Eastern Europe, there's one way in which Hungarians are similar to people in those other countries: their funerals still tend to incorporate many of the old traditions, long after they might be expected to have died out. One of these Hungarian death rituals includes opening all of the doors and windows in a house when death is imminent, to allow the soul to leave the house, but shutting the closet doors after death to prevent the soul from hiding there.

After death occurs, the family washes and dresses the body, usually in the one article of clothing that was saved for special occasions. They set the body in the casket in the parlor, or the front room of the house, and then proceed to eat a multicourse meal called "the last supper," usually in the next room. A wake follows, and wine and liquor flow freely.

The body is usually buried the next day, and after the last shovelful of dirt is tamped down onto the casket, the family sets up a table in the graveyard, where they serve sweet pastries and wine to the mourners. Afterward, the mourners return to the home of the deceased and partake in a full funeral feast: Funeral Goulash, a variation of standard goulash, is often served.

Fasting also plays a role in Hungarian mourning rituals; the immediate family is expected to fast on the birthday of the deceased as well as the anniversary of the death.

In medieval times, drinking cups and vessels were often made from lead. When someone drank ale or whiskey from the lead cup, the alcohol would react with the lead, and he would pass out as if he had drunk ten times as much. If he happened to pass out on the road, a villager passing by would drag him to his house, prepare him for burial, and then wait a few days until he woke up. Or didn't. This is one explanation for how the term "wake" came about.

Funeral Goulash

1 5-pound beef shoulder,
cut into 2-inch cubes
½ cup Hungarian
paprika
4 yellow onions,
chopped
2 heads garlic, peeled
and minced
1 cup fat from top
of brown stock
(see below)
8 large russet potatoes,
peeled and diced
2½ quarts brown stock
Salt and freshly ground
black pepper
1 pound dried egg
noodles
4 tablespoons unsalted
butter

Preheat the oven to 350°F.

In a large roasting pan, roll the beef chunks in the paprika, making sure all the surfaces are coated. Push the meat to one side. Repeat with the onions and garlic.

In a small saucepan, melt the fat from the brown stock. Add to the roasting pan and toss to coat well.

Place the roasting pan in the oven and loosely cover with foil. Brown the meat, stirring every 10 minutes so the meat browns evenly, for 20 to 30 minutes.

When the meat is browned, transfer it to a heavy stockpot and add the potatoes. Place over medium heat. Add the brown stock and bring to a boil. Decrease the heat to low and simmer. Occasionally skim the fat and scum from the surface and stir gently. Cook until the meat is tender, about 30 minutes. Add salt and pepper to taste. While the meat is cooking, prepare the noodles according to package instructions. Drain and return the noodles to the pot. Add the butter and stir well to combine.

Serve the meat with the buttered noodles.

SERVES 10

A
DMITTEDLY, LIFE IS DIFFICULT in a land where people live in total darkness for several months each year. Death isn't terribly easy for Icelanders, either. Up until the start of the twentieth century, killing the oldest and/or weakest members of a tribe or family was a common event. In medieval times, when famine, war, or an invading army struck, Icelanders would be forced to migrate. Often the oldest—and sometimes the youngest—would be left behind so that the others wouldn't be slowed down on their journey.

As one observer put it, "Men ate ravens and foxes, and many loathsome things were eaten which should not be eaten, and some men had the old and helpless killed and thrown over the cliffs."

As a result of the almost constant stress through the millennia, it's no surprise that Icelanders developed some unusual beliefs surrounding death, particularly when it

> ## A Culinary Epitaph, Take Three
>
> OH, CRUEL DEATH
> TO SATISFY THY PALATE,
> CUT DOWN OUR LETTUCE
> TO MAKE A SALAD.
>
> —*Epitaph for Lettuce Manning*

came to ghosts. When a stubborn ghost just wouldn't leave a family alone, they would take matters into their own hands. They'd open the grave, decapitate the corpse, and place the head under the buttocks. That way, the ghost wouldn't be able to figure out which way to go to continue to haunt the family, and, the belief goes, would just give up.

Icelanders eat a lot of fish. They also have a lot of holidays, probably to keep from going crazy. One of their holidays celebrates the death of St. Thorlakur Thorhallsson, a bishop of Skálholt, who died on December 23, 1193, which just happens to fall near the winter solstice. Many Icelanders celebrate both the shortest day of the year and the saint's death day by eating the fish known as skate.

Fried Skate

4 tablespoons all-
  purpose flour
1 pinch salt
1 pinch freshly ground
  black pepper
2 pounds skate or
  Icelandic flounder
  fillets, cut into
  6 pieces
3 tablespoons safflower
  oil
3 tablespoons unsalted
  butter
1/3 cup finely chopped
  hazelnuts or pecans
1 1/2 cups dry white wine
1 lemon, cut into
  6 wedges, for garnish

In a shallow dish, mix the flour, salt, and pepper together. Lightly coat the fish pieces in the flour. Cut a crosshatch pattern into the flesh of the fish, but not through the skin.

Heat the oil in a large sauté pan over medium-high heat. Add the fish and sauté for three minutes on each side. Transfer the fish to a serving platter. Loosely cover with foil. Drain the excess oil from the pan.

In the same pan, melt the butter over medium heat. Sauté the nuts until lightly toasted, about 5 minutes. Add the wine and continue to cook until the liquid is reduced by half. Pour the sauce over the fish and garnish with lemon wedges.

SERVES 6

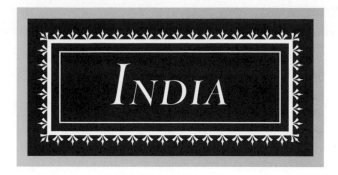

I^'s VIRTUALLY IMPOSSIBLE TO DESCRIBE a typical funeral or funeral feast in India, simply because of the diversity of religious and ethnic groups that call the subcontinent home, including Hindus, Buddhists, Muslims, Christians, and Zoroastrians. Each of these groups has its own unique methods of mourning; some are described elsewhere in this book.

However, among some of the different tribes of northern India, funeral rituals from various religions and ethnicities have been combined to create a unique funeral custom. One is from the Muslim tribe known as the Badaga sect.

In the Badaga culture, even if a person who's on his deathbed has no appetite and is physically incapable of swallowing, the Badagas will force him to eat. When the family determines that death is imminent, they will dip a coin in butter and place it in the mouth of the dying person. They call this the rite of *hana benne* (coin butter). It is necessary, the Badagas believe, because the person will need this coin to buy food and drink as well as the tolls he'll need to pay on his journey to the afterlife; the butter will provide him with strength for the trip. Without it, the tribe believes that he will not be allowed to enter heaven, and that will bring dishonor to the surviving family members.

Of course, many people on their deathbeds are liable to choke on the coin, which then brings on death even more quickly than it would have arrived otherwise. As a result, some members of the Badaga tribe have slightly altered the *hana benne* custom, and instead place the buttered coin in the mouth immediately after it's clear that the person is dead.

If you choose carrots that are approximately the diameter of a quarter, you'll be able to imagine that this dish is a bowl full of buttered coins. For added authenticity, you can carve narrow ridges along the length of the carrot before slicing to simulate the edge of a coin.

Buttered Carrot "Coins" with Lentils

1 pound dried lentils

½ cup (1 stick)
    unsalted butter

1 yellow onion, minced

2 large carrots, peeled
    and thinly sliced

1 pinch ground cloves

1 teaspoon minced flat-
    leaf parsley

¼ teaspoon freshly
    ground black pepper

Rinse the lentils and soak them in water overnight. Drain.

In a large, heavy stockpot, melt 1 tablespoon of the butter. Sauté the onion and carrot until the onion is translucent. Add the cloves, parsley, drained lentils, and pepper, with enough water to cover.

Cook over low heat until the lentils are tender, about 1½ hours. Just before serving, stir in the remaining butter.

SERVES 6

I N MANY INDONESIAN COMMUNITIES, once a death occurs the corpse is placed in a kind of giant sieve, which is hooked up to a pot that will slowly fill up with all of the various liquids that the body starts to emit once it reaches an advanced state of decomposition.

While the corpse is draining, which is known as the "wet" stage, Indonesians believe that the person lying in the casket isn't 100 percent dead; instead, they say he's "in transition." (Try and keep a straight face the next time you hear somebody say they're "in transition.") During the wet stage, the body is kept either inside the family's home or in a separate building nearby.

Once the body ceases to drain, it formally enters the "dry" stage; it is removed from its proximity to the living and placed nearer to the family's other dead relatives. At this point, the person is declared to be fully dead, and the survivors begin to refer to the person as an ancestor.

Other tribes throughout Indonesia follow a variety of other customs: for one, see the section on the Toraja tribe (page 142). They also put their dead through a transition process, although it doesn't involve an elaborate drainage apparatus. Instead, the corpse is dressed in street clothes and regularly offered food—presumably his favorite (or maybe his least favorite, if the surviving spouse has a grudge to bear)—in a separate building known as a *tongkonan*.

My favorite custom occurs among the Manggarai tribe of the Flores region. They believe dead people live in a place called Mori Karaeng. The dead only hang out with the living for five days before heading for Mori Karaeng, where everything is the total opposite of what they enjoyed—or hated—in life. As a result, the survivors smash plates, dishes, and cups on the fifth day so that the deceased will have utensils and plates to use in the next world. Whether or not you smash plates at a funeral, the spice in this Indonesian dessert will let you know you're alive.

Spicy Pineapple Salad
(Rujak Nanas)

1 pineapple

1 cucumber, peeled and sliced

1 tablespoon shrimp paste

6 birdseye chile peppers, chopped

3 tablespoons sugar

Salt

1 ½ tablespoons white vinegar

Peel and core the pineapple and cut into 1-inch chunks. In a large bowl, combine the pineapple with the cucumber slices. In a small bowl, combine the shrimp paste, chiles, sugar, salt, and vinegar. Sprinkle this mixture over the pineapple and cucumber. Mix well. Adjust the taste by adding more sugar, salt, or vinegar. Chill for at least two hours before serving.

SERVES 8

W HEN IT COMES TO DEATH, Iranians are extremely superstitious. If a dog barks just after sunrise, they believe that the angel of death is near the house; the family then rushes to block the door with an upside-down shoe to prevent the angel from entering. If an owl in a nearby tree hoots loudly, that also means death will soon visit the family inside the house.

But Iranians believe they have the power to counteract the message of the animals, partly through the use of food. The head of the household will hold a mirror up to the hooting owl and offer it some salt; this turns the owl into a bearer of good news instead of bad. And if two people living in the same house die within a short period, the remaining family members sacrifice a hen with black feathers and give it to a poor family in the village to prevent any more deaths from occurring.

> A mixture of bones in beer makes those who drink it cruel.
>
> —PHILIPPE ARIES

If, however, death arrives despite their best efforts, Iranians will still put a positive spin on it. When telling others about the death, they will say, "He has given his share of life to you," which implies that everyone will live just a bit longer due to their neighbor's unfortunate passing.

Iran is an Islamic country, which means that burial must be prompt. The Koran is read during the ritual washing of the body, and on the following day during the service and at the graveside. After the body is removed from the deathbed, the family places a brick on the deathbed, and then lays a slab of meat on top of it. Later, after the burial, the family sets some sweet syrup and halvah in the deathbed room. In the morning, the food is taken to the grave and the meat is distributed to the poor. Mourners also place food and drink next to the grave, to nourish the deceased on his journey.

Iranian Barley Soup

1 cup barley

1/2 cup lentils

6 cups water

2 yellow onions,
   chopped

2 tablespoons olive oil

1 tablespoon dried mint

1 teaspoon turmeric

1/2 teaspoon freshly
   ground black pepper

In a large stockpot, combine the barley, lentils, water, onions, olive oil, mint, turmeric, and pepper and bring to a boil. Decrease the heat and cover. Simmer for 1 hour, stirring occasionally, until the lentils are tender.

SERVES 6

*When I die I want to decompose in a barrel of porter and have it served
in all the pubs in Dublin. I wonder if they would know it was me?*

— J. P. DONLEAVY

IRISH FUNERALS ARE SO NOTORIOUS around the world that there are several web sites devoted to doing it right, including www.irishfuneral.com. Of course, the primary food group featured at an Irish funeral is booze. The best way to describe how it is used at an Irish funeral is with the following joke:

Paddy was on his deathbed, and his lifelong friend Thomas was sitting with him.

"Paddy, my friend," said Thomas, "do you remember that case of whiskey we won at poker about ten years ago?"

> At no time are the laws of hospitality more rigorously maintained than at the funeral feast.
>
> —BERTRAM S. PUCKLE

"Aye, Thomas, I do," said Paddy. "It was some very fine whiskey."

"Well," said Thomas, "I never told you, but I took one bottle and set it aside. I still have it."

Paddy's mouth started to water as he thought of the fine whiskey.

"Ah, Thomas, would you grant me one last favor, in the name of our friendship?"

"Anything, Paddy, what will it be?"

"When I'm gone and they put me in the ground and cover me with sod, will you pull the cork from that fine bottle of whiskey and pour it over my grave?"

"Paddy, you know I'll do anything for you," Thomas said, then paused. "But would you mind if it passes through my kidneys first?"

Of course, with all that alcohol, a groaning board of food has always been necessary to help absorb some of it, so the drinking could continue through the night. One of the old reliable comestibles is a Wake Cake.

Irish Wake Cake

3/4 cup (1 1/2 sticks)
   unsalted butter, at
   room temperature
1 cup sugar
2 teaspoons vanilla
   extract
2 large eggs
1 3-ounce package
   cream cheese, at room
   temperature
1 3/4 cups cake flour,
   sifted
1 1/4 teaspoons baking
   powder
1/4 teaspoon salt
1 cup dried currants
2/3 cup buttermilk

GLAZE

1/2 cup confectioners'
   sugar, sifted
2 teaspoons freshly
   squeezed lemon juice

Preheat the oven to 325°F. Grease and flour a 9-inch loaf pan.

With an electric mixer or by hand, cream the butter, sugar, and vanilla until fluffy. Add the eggs, one at a time, beating until fluffy. Add the cream cheese and blend until well combined.

In another bowl, sift the flour, baking powder, and salt together. Place the currants in a small bowl. Add 1/4 cup of the flour mixture to the currants and stir until the currants are well coated.

Alternately add one-third of the remaining flour mixture and one-third of the buttermilk to the batter, mixing well after each addition. Blend until smooth. Add the currants and stir until well distributed.

Pour the batter into the prepared pan. Bake until a tester comes out clean, about 1 hour and 25 minutes.

Transfer to a rack and let the cake rest in the pan for 10 minutes. Carefully remove the cake from the pan to the rack.

In a small bowl, combine the confectioners' sugar with the lemon juice and drizzle over the warm cake. Let the cake cool completely before serving.

SERVES 10

ISLAM

L IKE CHRISTIANITY, Islam covers a broad spectrum of ethnic groups and cultures, so it is impossible to generalize how food is regarded in the funeral practices of Turks, Egyptians, Moroccans, Lebanon, and so on. In fact, *Death Warmed Over: The Islam Story* could fill another entire book, if not two.

Certain customs, however, are common to most Muslims, and many of these involve food. A Muslim must be buried as soon as possible, no more than twenty-four hours after death. After burial, given the brief time between death and burial and the accompanying chaos, mourners gather at the family's home to pray for the deceased and read the Koran. Halvah, a sweet sesame paste candy, is usually passed out to guests as they leave the house.

The third, seventh, and fortieth days after the death of a Muslim, as well as the first anniversary, are considered to be significant. Muslims say prayers known as *mevlit* on these important days, either at home or at a mosque.

Shopping List

One medieval funeral feast in the year 1309 required of the following list of ingredients: Five pigs, one hare, five sheep, thirteen hens, nineteen geese, 1½ gallons of oysters, nine capons, 1½ carcasses of beef, wine, ale, eggs, bread, and fifty pounds of wax (for candles). The poor merely received a roll and a liquor concoction known as "dog's nose," a combination of rum and ale.

After *mevlit* is completed, usually in the afternoon, the family and mourners prepare to eat a hearty meal. More halvah and other sweets like *lokum*, which Westerners know as Turkish Delight, are given to guests on these anniversaries as well.

Halvah

1 15-ounce can tahini
   (sesame butter)
1 cup (2 sticks)
   margarine
4 cups all-purpose flour
1 cup honey
1/2 cup hulled sesame
   seeds
3 1-ounce squares semi-
   sweet chocolate

Drain the oil from the can of tahini into a glass measuring cup. Melt the margarine in a medium saucepan and add to the oil from the tahini to the level of approximately 1 1/2 cups. Return this mixture to the saucepan over a low flame and add the flour, stirring constantly. Cook, stirring often, until the mixture turns the color of caramel. Add the tahini and combine until smooth. Remove from the heat.

In a separate pot with a candy thermometer, heat the honey to the soft ball stage, 235°F, or when a drop of the honey dropped in a glass of cold water will form a soft ball that you can flatten with your fingers when it is taken out of the water.

Add the honey to the flour mixture, then add the sesame seeds. Mix well.

Grease a 9 by 13-inch baking dish. Press the halvah mixture into the dish and spread evenly.

Melt the chocolate in a double boiler. Pour the melted chocolate over the halvah and let cool.

MAKES 2 1/2 POUNDS

YOU MAY THINK THAT YOU KNOW everything there is to know about Italian-American funeral cuisine—New Jersey–style, of course—from watching *The Sopranos*, or even by leafing through a copy of *The Sopranos Family Cookbook*, but think again: in the series, although there are frequent scenes in restaurants and Carmela's kitchen, as well as at least a couple of visits each season to the local mob funeral home, the two worlds never quite meet up at the same time.

Like the bereaved in other cultures, the mourners in Italian villages often place cherished items in the casket with the deceased; these may include everything from candy and cigarettes to jars of antipasti. If the family inadvertently forgets to place something in the casket, when the next villager dies, the first family will ask the newly mourning family to place the item in their loved one's casket, figuring it will eventually reach the hands of the one who died first. Of course, that assumes that they're both heading to the same place.

> ## A Culinary Epitaph, Take Four
>
> WORMS ARE BAIT FOR FISH
> BUT HERE'S A SUDDEN CHANGE,
> FISH IS BAIT FOR WORMS,
> IS NOT THAT PASSING STRANGE?
> *—Epitaph for a Mister Fish*

Even if olives and artichoke hearts were favorite foods of the deceased, those family members left behind would probably be better off keeping any jars of these pickled Italian vegetables for themselves, since one old Italian funeral custom prohibited women from lighting a fire in the house for a full year after the death of a family member. That meant no heat and no cooking. Another custom forbade men from shaving for a year; one suspects they had it a lot easier than their wives, who must have become quite inventive with cold antipasto platters.

Italian Antipasto

1 6.5-ounce can Italian
 tuna fish in olive oil
4 thin slices Italian
 salami
4 thin slices prosciutto
4 anchovy fillets, drained
2 celery hearts, cut in
 half lengthwise
8 large green olives
8 large black olives
2 teaspoons capers
4 artichoke hearts in oil
1 4-ounce can pimientos
1 medium tomato, sliced
4 pepperoncini
1 large loaf crusty
 Italian bread
1/2 cup (1 stick) unsalted
 butter

On a large oval platter, set the tuna fish in the center and arrange all the other ingredients except the bread and butter around it. Place the bread in a basket alongside, with the butter.

SERVES 4

JAMAICA

To foreigners, funerals in Jamaica must look like outright celebrations, in part because the natives are deathly afraid of ghosts. I'll explain: Many Jamaicans believe that the good soul of a deceased person automatically travels to Africa immediately after death, while a bad soul tends to stick around, languishing around cotton trees on the island and generally bringing negative energy to those still alive. Therefore, not only is a raucous, celebratory wake supposed to celebrate the life of the deceased, but if the bad soul is inclined to hang around, the good cheer will essentially disable the evil, creating a relatively passive ghost.

A Jamaican wake is referred to as Nine Nights. The lengthy party allows enough time for the soul to escape the body and head for its next destination. For nine nights after the burial, family and friends set a plate of fried fish and cake inside a tent next to the house so the dead can eat. They then dance and drink and sing loudly until midnight. After nine nights the soul, thus fortified, is ready to make its trip. Then, forty nights after the death, another party is held. Although it is assumed that the soul has found its way by then, another night of dancing and singing is held just to make sure—and besides, the thinking goes, it can't hurt.

> ### A Culinary Epitaph, Take Five
>
> Throughout his life he kneaded bread
> And deemed it quite a bore.
> But now six feet beneath earth's crust
> He needeth bread no more.
>
> —*Epitaph for a baker*

Some Jamaicans also place several johnnycakes—the original term was *journey cake*—in the casket with the deceased just before burial to make sure that the soul has enough food for the journey.

Johnnycake

1 cup yellow cornmeal

1 1/2 cups milk

1/2 cup butter, at room
   temperature

1/2 cup sugar

1 1/3 cups pastry flour

2 1/2 teaspoons baking
   powder

1 teaspoon salt

1 egg

Preheat the oven to 350°F. Grease an 8-inch square pan. In a large mixing bowl, combine the cornmeal and 1/2 cup of the milk. Set aside.

In another bowl, cream the butter and gradually add the sugar. Set aside.

In another bowl, sift the flour, baking powder, and salt together. In a glass measuring cup, beat together the egg and the remaining 1 cup milk. Alternately add the flour mixture and the milk/egg mixture to the butter mixture, stirring after each addition until combined. Add the cornmeal mixture and mix until smooth.

Pour into the prepared pan and bake for 45 minutes. Cut into nine squares and serve hot with butter and syrup, if desired.

MAKES 9 SQUARES

I N MANY JAPANESE VILLAGES, although visitors frequently bring food to the home where someone is on his deathbed, it is anathema to cook it. So instead, it is served raw. Perhaps because of an ancient belief about cooking the life out of food, it is thought that heating a meal in the house will only hasten an impending death. After the person dies, however, the women in the household proceed to cook enough rice and vegetables to feed an entire village. Curiously, it is forbidden to serve fish at the funeral feast.

Japan is primarily a Buddhist country, so upon death a Buddhist wake known as a *tsuya* is held at the family home. A monk conducts the service while a photograph of the deceased is placed on the family altar along with a bowl of rice with a pair of chopsticks standing vertically in the bowl.

The funeral is usually held the day after the death; the body is cremated immediately after the funeral. It is actually against the law in Japan to bury an intact body, though ashes and, presumably, body parts can be buried. Once the body is cremated, mourners use chopsticks to separate the bones from the ashes and place them in a special urn. Afterward, a funeral meal known as an *otoki* is offered by relatives; before the guests leave, the family sprinkles some salt on the mourners' shoulders to remove the threat of death from their lives.

Much like Mexico's Day of the Dead is the Japanese Obon, a three-day period in midsummer during which dead relatives are believed to return to their ancestral lands, and it's up to the living to ensure that they leave happy. The days leading up to Obon are hectic ones, with relatives cleaning not only the graves of the returning ancestors, but their houses, too, and preparing food offerings for the cemetery and for the Buddhist altar at home.

One Obon custom is to carve an eggplant into the shape of a horse and place it by the grave on the last night of the festival so the deceased relatives can quickly make their way back to the afterworld when the festival ends. You can try your hand at carving an eggplant, or you can just make the following recipe.

Japanese Eggplant with Sesame-Ginger Glaze

1 tablespoon rice-wine or cider vinegar

1 tablespoon soy sauce

1 tablespoon hoisin sauce

3 tablespoons sesame oil

1 tablespoon sugar

2 tablespoons minced fresh ginger

3 cloves garlic, minced

8 small Japanese eggplants, 1/4 pound each, halved length-wise

1 teaspoon salt

1 teaspoon freshly ground black pepper

2 green onions, minced

In a small bowl, whisk together the vinegar, soy sauce, hoisin sauce, sesame oil, sugar, ginger, and garlic. Use a pastry brush to spread the glaze over the eggplants, reserving about half for later steps. Sprinkle with the salt and pepper.

Set the barbecue grill to medium heat. Place the eggplant, cut side down, on the grill and cook for 5 minutes. Turn the eggplant and brush with the glaze. Cook until the eggplant softens. Transfer the eggplant to a serving platter and drizzle with more glaze. Sprinkle with minced green onions and serve.

SERVES 4

My grandfather had a wonderful funeral. It was held in a big hall with accordion players. On the buffet table there was a replica of the deceased in potato salad.—WOODY ALLEN

JEWISH LAW DICTATES THAT the body of the deceased is to be buried no more than twenty-four hours after the moment of death, providing a very narrow window in which to throw together a decent buffet; indeed, the lack of time means that food is not a major consideration at most Jewish funerals. Instead, the post-funeral period known as sitting *shiva* is when some serious feasting gets done.

One Jewish acquaintance describes *shiva* as a pretty somber affair, aside from the eating. "*Shiva* is a seven-day orgy of eating," is how he put it. The immediate family spends the week at home sitting on wooden boxes (this is no time to be comfortable) with all mirrors in the house covered (this is no time for vanity), indulging in the platters of deli food that visitors bring on an almost hourly basis (this is no time to be cooking).

Before *shiva* starts, and just after the mourners return from the cemetery, the prescribed meal consists of hard-boiled eggs and salt: the eggs represent the regeneration of life, while the salt stands for absolute incorruptibility. Another Jewish acquaintance who grew up in the shadows of New York's Russian-Jewish mob in the 1960s described funerals for his rougher relatives at which the eggs were boiled twice as long as needed and dunked in so much salt that they resembled salt licks. He surmises that these excesses were attempts by the deceased's colleagues to offer up some kind of restitution for the deceased's past sins, thus rendering the soul more pure in the eyes of God.

These same funerals, he notes, often broke with Jewish tradition by turning into all-day affairs at the local kosher deli or Jewish catering hall immediately after the burial. Some families even held an abbreviated form of *shiva* at the restaurant, holding court alongside the tables topped with Sterno-heated buffet dishes for several days. Mourners could then drop by at their leisure—or when they had made no previous dinner plans—to pay their respects to the immediate family for an hour or two, and grab a plate full of knishes, blintzes, and latkes before heading home.

Potato Latkes

*4 large russet potatoes,
   peeled and quartered*

*3 large yellow onions,
   peeled and quartered*

3 eggs

*1 1/2 teaspoons kosher
   salt*

*1/2 teaspoon white
   pepper*

*2 teaspoons baking
   powder*

*1/2 teaspoon baking
   soda*

1/3 cup unbleached flour

Canola oil for frying

Shred the potatoes in a food processor fitted with a fine blade. Shred the onions. Remove the bowl and cover from the processor and transfer the mixture to a colander. Press down firmly to drain out the liquid.

Put the potato mixture in a large bowl. Add the eggs, salt, pepper, baking powder, and baking soda and stir thoroughly. Stir in the flour. Set aside.

Set a large frying pan over medium-high heat. Pour in the oil to a depth of 1/2 inch. When the oil is hot, add large tablespoonfuls of the potato mixture to the pan. Cook the latkes until golden on the bottom. Flip them over and cook until done. Drain on paper towels and cook the rest of the batter, stirring the batter before each batch.

MAKES 24 LATKES

KOREA

A

S IN OTHER ASIAN CULTURES, when a Korean man, woman, or child dies, rice plays an important role in the mourning rituals. But rice is not only used as a part of the funeral feast and the menu served during the wake; it's also used as a prop for the soul.

Upon a death, the family throws uncooked rice onto the roof or sets a bowl of it outside the front door, to encourage the bad spirit of death to take its leave as quickly as possible and not take any of the family members who are still alive. A pair of shoes made out of rice straw is part of the traditional mourning outfit for women.

> Orthodox Jews once made their coffins from the boards of a table at which the poor had been fed.

During burial at the cemetery, a mourner holds a wooden box open over the grave while the coffin is lowered into the ground. At the same time, another mourner repeats the name of the deceased. This is to capture the soul in the box. The "box of soul" is then presented to the family, in much the same way as a folded-up American flag is presented to the family of a U.S. veteran at the cemetery. The family keeps the box for a year and lets it participate in most family activities at home, including mealtimes—although you have to wonder how active a participant it can be in games of mah-jongg or even light conversation. The family sets food offerings in front of the box at breakfast and dinner; then, at the end of the year, the family burns the box in a ceremony, at which time the soul is released and heads for heaven.

In addition, for three months after the death, members of the immediate family visit the grave on the first and fifteenth day of each month and lay food by the grave. The hundredth day after the death marks the end of the mourning period.

Kimchi—aka fermented cabbage—is the unofficial national dish of Korea. Here's a variation on the theme: Kimchi Stew, perfect to bring to a family in mourning.

Kimchi Stew

½ pound boneless pork chop

1 14-ounce jar kimchi, drained

3 tablespoons canola oil

3 cups water

1 12-ounce package fresh tofu, cut into 1-inch chunks

4 dried shiitake mushrooms, soaked in water

2 green onions, chopped

Cut the pork into ½-inch cubes. Drain the kimchi, reserving the liquid.

In a saucepan, heat the oil over medium-high heat. Add the pork and cook until almost done. Stir in the drained kimchi. Cook for 5 minutes, stirring constantly.

Add the reserved kimchi liquid and the water. Turn the heat to high and bring to a boil. Remove from the heat and add the tofu, mushrooms, and green onion. Let stand for 5 minutes before serving.

SERVES 4

I N COUNTLESS AIRINGS OF *A Prairie Home Companion,* Garrison Keillor reverently details the joys of a Lutheran church supper to which all the relatives of the Norwegian bachelor farmers were expected to bring a Hot Dish. It took many years before I figured out that he was talking about what we, growing up in New Jersey, referred to as the elegant French import, *le casserole.*

I've never heard Mr. Keillor refer to it as a Funeral Hot Dish, however. Those in the Hot Dish Brigade usually synchronize plans in advance so that the requisite offerings of Jell-O mold with marshmallows and maraschino cherries—known as the salad course—prepackaged rolls, cold cuts, and Hot Dishes are in the correct proportions. Sometimes, due to the short notice of a post-funeral luncheon or supper, some are caught unprepared, and instead must rely on the funeral home or caterer to prepare the meal.

> Italians . . . seemed never to die. They eat olive oil all day long . . . and that's what does it.
>
> —WILLIAM KENNEDY

Good Lutherans would consider that a travesty and an insult to the memory of the deceased in whose honor the meal is served. The serious Hot Dish Brigade always has provisions at the ready in well-stocked pantries; they are ready to drop everything and, ninety minutes after hanging up the phone at the news, head out the door with one Hot Dish in potholdered hands—to bring to the grieving family's home—and a second Hot Dish set out to cool for the funeral luncheon later on.

Anything less would be frowned upon where Hot Dish church suppers are weekly events, and where more than one church member has asked to be buried with a fork in his hand.

Funeral Hot Dish

1 pound ground beef

1 yellow onion, chopped

1 pound macaroni,
cooked, drained, and
cooled

1 10½-ounce can
condensed tomato
soup

1 14-ounce can corn,
drained

1 14-ounce can chopped
tomatoes

Salt and freshly ground
black pepper

4 slices of American
cheese

Preheat the oven to 325°F. In a large saucepan over medium heat, brown the ground beef and onion. Grease a four-quart casserole dish. Add the cooked beef, onion, macaroni, soup, corn, tomatoes, and salt and pepper to taste. Mix well. Top with the cheese slices and bake for 30 minutes.

SERVES 8

MADAGASCAR

WITH EIGHTEEN DIFFERENT TRIBES recognized by the government the island nation of Madagascar, in the Indian Ocean, is considered by anthropologists rich with potential for multicultural study. French, Polynesian, and Arabic rituals all influence the tribes, which makes for a unique mix of funeral customs. The Merina tribe lives in straw and palm huts; their dead relatives live in elaborate stone tombs, usually carved in the side of a mountain. Burials are communal; when a member dies, the body is placed in the tomb with previously deceased relatives.

Merina funerals largely resemble polka parties (for more reasons than one) in the event they call a *famadihana*. The celebration is held before the body is buried but after the communal tomb is opened. During the *famadihana*, members of the tribe remove skeletal remains from the tomb and dance with them, sit them down at the table to eat, and even take them back to the hut where they lived when they were alive. Also during the party, some of the bones are taken from the tomb, combined with others in a large pit, and ground together, much like using a mortar and pestle, before wrapping them in a linen cloth and replacing them in the tomb. No mention is made of how the tribe selects whose bones are to be ground, but one anthropologist who has observed more than a few *famadihana* among the Merina has noted that the predominant tune played during the grinding phase of the party is "Roll Out the Barrel." In fact, music plays a vital role in Madagascar funerals. Another tribal custom dictates that after the body is laid in the tomb, a portable radio is placed next to the body. Before the stone is replaced at the door to the tomb, the radio is turned on, probably to a polka station.

A Culinary Epitaph, Take Six

THIS IS ON ME, BOYS!

—*Epitaph for a bartender*

Polka music means beer, so if you don't have a funeral to use as an excuse to drink beer, use a pinch of sakay, a Madagascar spice mixture—the red pepper will be enough of an excuse.

Sakay

1/2 cup crushed red
  pepper flakes
1 tablespoon ground
  ginger
2 cloves garlic, finely
  minced
4 tablespoons peanut
  oil

In a small bowl, stir together the pepper flakes, ginger, and garlic until combined. Add the oil, 1 tablespoon at a time, and mix with the pepper mixture until thoroughly combined. Place in a bowl and set on the table to use as a condiment.

MAKES 2/3 CUP

Maori

BEFORE THE NINETEENTH CENTURY, the Maori of New Zealand believed that a person was not completely dead until the body was 100 percent decomposed, with only bones left over. In fact, if any flesh was still on the bones, it was scraped off during a special ceremony, the *hahunga*. Only then were the bones buried.

Today, like peoples of many cultures with ancient traditions, the Maori incorporate certain elements of their ancient practices into their funeral services, although they no longer scrape the bones. In fact, a corpse is usually buried three days after death. Once the mourners return home from the cemetery, they conduct a *tapu* ceremony, in which they thoroughly wash up to remove all traces of the malevolent spirit of death.

Then the party and great funeral feast, or *tangi*, begin, usually fortified with plenty of alcohol. The entire village pitches in to prepare enough food and drink for hundreds of people, since they allow anyone to attend, even if the guest had never met the deceased or any of the surviving relatives. The main attraction of the feast is typically a roast pig that is laid out on the ground; guests sit down around it and pluck meat from the pig with their fingers.

> ## Death of a Hen
>
> The little hen choked on a nut. The cock ran to seek help, but when he returned, the hen had already died. Six mice pulled her funeral carriage, but they slipped into a stream and drowned. The little cock dug her a grave, then he sat down and mourned until he died.
>
> —THE DEATH OF THE LITTLE HEN, BROTHERS GRIMM

However, in some cases, the Maori mourners may start the *tangi* before the burial and keep the casket in the village for the sole purpose of lengthening the duration of the funeral feast.

Rewena Paraoa (Maori Bread)

1 cup water

½ russet potato, peeled and thickly sliced

7 cups all-purpose flour

1 teaspoon sugar

1 teaspoon salt

1 teaspoon baking soda

In a saucepan, bring the water to a boil. Place the potato slices in the water and continue to boil until soft. Cool to lukewarm and add 2 cups of the flour and the sugar. Mix until it forms a paste. Cover and set in a warm place until the mixture has fermented.

Preheat the oven to 350°F. Grease two loaf pans. Sift the remaining 5 cups flour and salt into a large bowl and make a well in the center. Fill with the potato-flour mixture and sprinkle baking soda over the top. Combine and knead the mixture for about 10 minutes, adding a little water if the dough is too stiff. Place the dough in the greased loaf pans. Bake for 45 to 50 minutes, until the top is browned.

MAKES 2 LOAVES

OF THE MANY FUNERAL TRADITIONS throughout Mexico, the best-known post-funeral celebration is the Day of the Dead, also known as All Souls' Day, on November 2. Officially, it is the one day of the year when dead ancestors return to earth to visit. November 1 is All Saints' Day, and traditionally celebrations begin that evening, though in the daytime families tend to honor children who have died, reserving the evenings for adult ancestors.

On November 2, families spend the day at the cemetery where loved ones are buried. They clean the area around the grave, wash the tombstone, and place the deceased's favorite foods around the grave. Huge flower arrangements are also common. Most families also build a small altar—either at the gravesite or at the home or office—and place food offerings and favorite items on it as well

Food is also a central part of Day of the Dead celebrations for those still walking the earth. Special black plates and bowls are sold only during the last two weeks in October, and bakeries make hundreds of life-size skull-shaped cakes with the name of the deceased written in frosting on the forehead. In fact, candy and desserts—from chocolate caskets to candy skeletons—take center stage during the Day of the Dead. And like people of other cultures who save biscuits and cakes from the funeral as a memento of a lost loved one, many Mexicans will hold onto these candy bones for years.

Parlor Games

Until the early 1900s, the best room in most homes in North America was the parlor, whose main function was for laying out the dead for several days until burial. It was also known as the wake-room. However, once families began to use funeral homes—first called funeral *parlors,* perhaps to make them seem more home-like to a generation that had always cared for their own dead—in increasing numbers, the primary function of the parlor at home died out. Then, sometime in the 1940s, in an effort to distance the room from its earlier use, an industrious magazine columnist did a 180-degree turn and christened the parlor the "living room."

Pan de Muerto
(Bread of the Dead)

1/2 cup (1 stick)
   unsalted butter

1/2 cup milk

1/2 cup water

5 to 5 1/2 cups all-
   purpose flour

2 packages dry yeast

1 teaspoon salt

1 tablespoon whole
   anise seed

1 cup sugar

4 eggs

1/3 cup freshly squeezed
   orange juice

2 tablespoons grated
   orange zest

In a saucepan over a medium flame, heat the butter, milk, and water until the butter melts.

In a large mixing bowl, combine 1 1/2 cups of the flour, the yeast, salt, and anise seed, and 1/2 cup of the sugar. Add the butter and milk mixture and stir until well combined. Add the eggs and beat in another cup of flour. Continue to add more flour until the dough is soft but not sticky. Knead the dough on a lightly floured board for 10 minutes, or until smooth and elastic.

Lightly grease a large mixing bowl and place the dough in it. Cover with plastic wrap and let rise in a warm place until doubled in bulk, about 1 1/2 hours. Punch the dough down and shape into 2 loaves resembling skulls or skeletons. Let rise in a warm place for 1 hour.

Preheat the oven to 350°F. Bake the loaves on a baking sheet for 40 minutes, or until the tops are golden brown. While the bread is baking, prepare the glaze. In a small saucepan, mix the remaining 1/2 cup of sugar and the orange juice and zest over high heat. Bring to a boil, stirring constantly, for two minutes, then remove from the heat. Keep warm. When bread is done, apply the glaze to the hot loaves with a pastry brush.

MAKES 2 LOAVES

MONGOLIA

Prior to 1921, the people of Mongolia predominantly followed the tenets of Tibetan Buddhism, so the primary method of corpse disposal was to set it out for the wild dogs, wolves, and vultures that roamed the land. But before doing so, the Lamaist monks would determine which day of the week was the luckiest for the "air burial" of the deceased—Monday, Wednesday, or Friday. If the wild animals did a satisfactory job within three days—that is, there wasn't much left of the body—then local folk would be able to say that the deceased was a good person. If bits and scraps were still hanging off the bones, the soul was deemed to be bad, and the reputation of the surviving family members would suffer.

In 1921, when the local government was overthrown by the Chinese People's Revolutionary Party, all Lamaist activities were outlawed. This continued until 1990, when the country gave up socialism for good. Today, funeral ceremonies and burial rituals usually contain elements from each era.

Burial takes place within twenty-four hours of death, and the head of the deceased always points south. Once the body is in the ground, family and guests walk around the grave three times, pouring the fermented milk of a horse around the perimeter, ostensibly to fortify the soul for its impending journey. After the burial, mourners return to the home of the deceased, where the family serves a bowl of rice with raisins to each of the guests.

Don't Forget the Fix-o-dent!

People are always dropping last little things in [the casket]. They seem to see it as a journey to a foreign country where you may not be able to get some of the things you have here. I've seen the widow slide in a packet of his favorite digestive biscuits. Or it's the spare glasses and the set of false teeth. You wouldn't believe how many tubes of dental fixative go through here in a week.

—CREMATORIUM OPERATOR, QUOTED IN *GRAVE MATTERS*, BY NIGEL BARLEY

Rice Pudding with Raisins

2 eggs, beaten

4 cups milk

½ cup sugar

½ cup uncooked white
rice

1 tablespoon butter

1 teaspoon vanilla
extract

½ cup raisins

⅛ teaspoon ground
nutmeg

Preheat the oven to 300°F. Grease a 2-quart baking dish. In a medium bowl, beat the eggs and milk together. Add the sugar, rice, butter, vanilla extract, raisins, and nutmeg. Pour into the baking dish and bake for 2 to 2½ hours, stirring frequently during the first hour.

SERVES 6

MORMON

RUMOR HAS IT THAT THOSE who belong to the Church of Jesus Christ of Latter Day Saints—aka the Mormons—pride themselves on keeping a kind of secret society. They frequently refer to outsiders as NeverMos (Never Mormon) and Fornicators with a capital F.

One of the few things that Fornicators are allowed to know about the Mormon religion it that its believers are prohibited from partaking in alcohol, caffeine, and tobacco. Since that doesn't leave much, sugar appears frequently on the menu at any Mormon get-together. As one ex-Mormon put it, "If there's a way to put sugar in a recipe, Mormons will do it."

Excommunicated Mormons take pleasure in deriding some of the more entrenched Mormon customs, including the practice of calling any dish that contains Jell-O a "salad"; the popularity of a brisket recipe that calls for 12 cups of brown sugar (!); and the grand efforts of each church's Relief Society—the group of hardy women who arm themselves with spatulas to prepare mounds of grub to feed church members after worship, weddings, and funerals.

Ex-Mormons tell of post-funeral groaning boards running the length of the church meeting hall with not a free inch of space to be seen; the highlight of these feasts is the infinite variety of multicolored Jell-O dishes vying for attention. Although these Mormon salads typically contain fruit cocktail and are topped with Cool Whip, one ex-Mormon claims that one actually contained what appeared to be most of a box of Lucky Charms cereal.

In old Scotland, those preparing a body for burial would put a bell under the head of the corpse to announce his arrival, a salt cellar on the chest to symbolize immortality, and a loaf of bread under the arm to represent the mortal body.

One popular salad of choice, however, does not contain one speck of Jell-O. It's called Frog Eye Salad, after the small pasta bits mixed in. Despite the dearth of Jell-O, in this one, as in any good Mormon dish, sugar is still in ample supply.

1/2 cup sugar

1 tablespoon all-purpose flour

1/4 teaspoon salt

1 8-ounce can crushed pineapple in its own juice, undrained

1 20-ounce can chunk pineapple in its own juice, undrained

1 egg, beaten

2 teaspoons bottled lemon juice

8 ounces acini di pepe or orzo pasta, uncooked

3 1/2 cups (8 ounces) frozen nondairy whipped topping

2 11-ounce cans mandarin orange segments, drained

3 cups miniature marshmallows

1/2 cup sweetened flaked coconut

1 4-ounce jar maraschino cherries, drained

Frog Eye Salad

In a saucepan, stir together the sugar, flour, and salt.

Drain both cans of pineapple, reserving one cup of juice. Gradually stir the juice and egg into the sugar mixture. Cook over medium heat, stirring frequently, until the mixture comes to a boil. Add the lemon juice. Remove from the heat and let cool to room temperature.

Cook the pasta according to the package directions; drain. Rinse with cold water to cool quickly; drain again.

In large serving bowl, stir the cooled pineapple juice mixture together with the cooked pasta. Cover; refrigerate several hours or overnight.

Thaw the whipped topping according to the package directions. Add the crushed and chunk pineapple to the refrigerated mixture along with the oranges, two cups of the whipped topping, and the marshmallows and coconut. Mix gently and thoroughly. Cover; refrigerate until cold.

Just before serving, top with the remaining whipped topping and garnish with the cherries.

SERVES 12

MOROCCO

THE BERBERS—the predominant ethnic group in Morocco—are a nomadic people, so it makes sense that their food tends toward the portable variety, even when they're staying put. Visitors to the country often complain that the food choices are somewhat limited—either a stew known as a tagine or a kebab dish called brochettes—and if you want something off the beaten track you're better off heading north to Spain.

Because almost all Berbers follow the Islamic faith, their funerals are pretty simple: burial occurs as soon as possible after death, in a simple grave topped with a cairn of stones, and there are no flowers and no black clothes. Cemeteries in Morocco are mostly deserted except during funerals; otherwise, most families only visit their relatives' graves on the day of Holy Friday in the Muslim calendar.

Also in keeping with Islam, only men are allowed to attend funerals, for either men or women. Seven days after the funeral, the same men who attended the funeral serve a funeral feast for themselves in honor of the deceased. If a wife's husband dies, she does not go to the funeral but is compelled to wear a white dress while she mourns for forty days after the death. In some regions of the country, the widow is obliged to provide a funeral feast for all mourners, male and female, on the fortieth day after her husband's death.

3 tablespoons olive oi
plus more for brusk

1 whole chicken breas
boned and skinned

3 large onions, chopp

Salt and freshly grou
pepper

1 tablespoon coriande
seeds

2 tablespoons cinnam

1 teaspoon saffron
threads

1 teaspoon cumin see

1 teaspoon allspice

1 teaspoon ground clo

1 tablespoon grated
fresh ginger

1/2 cup canned chicken
broth

10 phyllo sheets

3 eggs and 1 egg yolk

1/2 cup blanched
almonds, toasted ar
chopped

1/2 teaspoon cinnamo

1 tablespoon confec-
tioners' sugar

Pastilla

In a large frying pan, heat the 3 table-spoons olive oil. Add the chicken and cook, turning, until browned. Add the onions, salt, pepper, and spices. Stir in the chicken broth. Cover and simmer for 40 to 45 minutes, until done, turning the chicken a few times while cooking. Add more broth if necessary.

Remove the chicken from the heat and let cool. Over medium heat, continue to simmer the cooking liquid until it is reduced by half. Cut the cooled chicken into bite-sized pieces.

Grease a springform pan and line it with nine of the phyllo sheets as follows: set one sheet on the bottom and lightly brush with olive oil. Arrange the other eight sheets so that they overlap the sides of the pan, lightly brushing each sheet with olive oil. Set aside.

Preheat the oven to 350°F. In a small bowl, beat the eggs and egg yolk together. Add to the sauce and cook over medium heat, stirring constantly, until it becomes creamy.

Place the chicken in the phyllo-lined pan. Top with the almonds and the sauce. Cover with the remaining phyllo sheet. Baste with oil.

Gather the edges of the overlapping sheets and bring them toward the middle over the cover sheet. Flatten the overlapping edges over the top sheet. Brush the top with oil. Bake for 45 minutes. Let stand for 10 minutes. Sprinkle with the cinnamon and sugar and serve.

SERVES 2

NEWFOUNDLAND

I THINK THAT WHEN I DIE, I want to have a funeral like the merry wakes that Newfoundlanders used to have up through the first half of the twentieth century. Most lasted for three days and two nights, and though the respectable came by the house to pay their respects in daylight, the fun really began once the sun set, the family retired for the night, and friends started the wake in the family's home while they slept. Based on the stories of pranks and other goings-on, however, it's difficult to believe that any of the family could have slept through the night.

Food was laid out and replenished at least several times during the night, and of course the alcohol flowed freely. Understandably, the presence of the dearly departed provided fodder for more than stories. Tales handed down tell of mourners attaching fishing line to a corpse's limbs to mimic a marionette, playing a hand of poker in which the deceased was expected to be an active participant, and propping up the dead body and supplying him with a glass of whatever libation was putting these wild ideas into his buddies' heads. The raucous activity would cease every four hours so the mourners could recite the rosary. Afterward, they'd pick up right where they'd left off.

In addition to food and liquor, other temptations were acted upon, mostly in an attempt to seem more alive than the body in the casket. A local midwife didn't need a calculator to compute the date of conception; all she had to do was listen for stories about a particularly boisterous merry wake—though you have to ask, was there any other kind?—and then know that her calendar would be full nine months hence. In fact, a rash of deaths usually resulted in an epidemic of births three seasons later. There's an oft-repeated saying among Newfy Catholics: An increase in the population nine months after a wake more than made up for the one death. Any food served during a merry wake couldn't be fragile, and it had to stand up to sitting out on the table for hours on end. Codfish Cakes fit the bill.

Codfish Cakes

1 pound salt cod,
soaked overnight in
water to cover,
drained, boned, and
skinned
1 pound russet potatoes,
peeled, cooked, and
mashed
4 tablespoons cream
1 bunch parsley,
chopped
1 tablespoon chopped
thyme
1 bunch scallion tops,
chopped
Salt and freshly ground
black pepper
Vegetable oil for frying
Flour for dusting

Cook the cod in simmering water for about 15 minutes. Drain and let dry and cool slightly.

In a large bowl, combine the cod, potatoes, cream, parsley, thyme, scallions, and salt and pepper to taste. Mix well. Form the mixture into twelve cakes.

In a large frying pan, heat 1/2 inch of oil. Lightly dust the cakes with flour and fry until golden on each side.

MAKES 12 CAKES

NEW ORLEANS
JAZZ FUNERAL

YOU MAY HAVE TO CHECK your calendar if you happen to stumble upon a New Orleans jazz funeral, because it's easy to mistake it for Mardi Gras in the French Quarter, although there's a casket with a real body inside. Jazz funerals in New Orleans are legendary events. Though a funeral is traditionally a melancholy and private family event, jazz funerals in the Big Easy are intended to be public events—at the very least, so that onlookers can contemplate their own mortality while enjoying the music and the spectacle.

Mourners who participate in the slow, plodding parade from the church to the cemetery will occasionally interrupt their strides with slightly jerky motions, a holdover from an African tradition that maintained these movements keep the malevolent spirits at bay. Actually, it's more of a dance than a walk, with colorful costumes and clothing instead of dour, dark outfits. Food, booze, and jazz bands accompany the procession, which is often led by a horse-drawn hearse and escorted by a coterie of New Orleans' finest, which may include drag queens, strippers, and musicians who just happen to be passing by and decide to join the party for an improvisational free-for-all.

At several monasteries in Germany and Italy, the monks mummify their deceased brothers, arranging them in a variety of positions in the burial vault in order to provide an accurate picture of everyday life at the monastery to (living) visitors. And so the mummified brothers are displayed performing a variety of tasks, including preparing a meal and sitting down to enjoy it.

One especially nice thing about the following recipe for Jambalaya is that you can start it in the morning before the funeral and it will be ready by the time you return home.

Funeral Jambalaya

2 cups boiled ham, diced

2 yellow onions,
    coarsely chopped

2 stalks celery, diced

1 green pepper, seeded
    and diced

1 28-ounce can whole
    tomatoes

1/4 cup tomato paste

3 cloves garlic, minced

1 tablespoon minced
    parsley

1/2 teaspoon dried thyme

2 whole cloves

2 tablespoons olive oil

1 cup long-grain
    converted rice,
    uncooked

1 pound fresh or frozen
    shrimp, uncooked,
    shelled and deveined

Place all ingredients except the shrimp in a large slow cooker. Mix well. Cover and cook on low for 8 to 10 hours.

Fifteen minutes before serving, increase the temperature to high. Add the shrimp and stir. Cover and cook until the shrimp are pink and tender, about 10 to 15 minutes.

SERVES 6

NORWAY

ON'T EVER ACCUSE A Norwegian of keeping his deceased loved ones
out of the loop. In Norway, some families create a kind of outdoor
screened room at the cemetery, directly over the graves of family
members. A canvas canopy serves as a roof, and a bench is set on
the mounded grave. Screening or mosquito netting is draped around tent posts
for added protection in summer. On special family occasions and holidays the family gathers at the gravesite and proceeds to bring everyone—even the deceased—up
to date on the family's activities as well as current world events. Many Norwegians
frequently bring a picnic along in order to
more pleasantly pass the time.

Though many cemeteries have
benches and stone monuments scattered
around the grounds for the use of
patrons, these items are considered to be
for public use, not for just one family.

There are several other Norwegian
funeral food rituals that differ somewhat

> **A Culinary Epitaph,
> Take Seven**
>
> PEAS TO HIS HASHES.
> (PEACE TO HIS ASHES.)
> —*Epitaph for a chef*

from those of other cultures. One old Norwegian custom calls for guests to
make a frosted cake, inscribe the initials of the deceased person into the frosting, and carry the cake in a wooden basket to the funeral. Afterward, each guest
gives their cake to the surviving head of the family, who sits at the door. The
cakes will make an appearance at the feast after the funeral, which includes
copious amounts of both coffee and wine.

Norwegian Funeral Cake

1 1/2 cups (3 sticks)
  unsalted butter,
  at room temperature

2 cups granulated
  sugar

3 eggs

1 1/2 cups sour cream

2 teaspoons vanilla
  extract

3 cups all-purpose flour

2 1/4 teaspoons baking
  powder

3/4 teaspoon baking
  soda

3/8 teaspoon salt

1 cup heavy cream

1/4 cup plus 1 table-
  spoon brown sugar

1/2 cup chopped walnuts

1/2 cup walnut halves

Preheat the oven to 350°F. Grease and flour three 9-inch round cake pans. With an electric mixer or by hand, cream the butter and sugar together in a large bowl. Beat in the eggs, one at a time, until the mixture is fluffy. Add the sour cream and 1 1/2 teaspoons of the vanilla and stir well. In a separate bowl, sift the flour, baking powder, baking soda, and salt together. Add to the creamed mixture and mix thoroughly.

Pour the batter into the prepared pans. Bake for 45 minutes, or until a tester comes out clean. Allow the layers to rest for 15 minutes in the pans, then turn out onto a rack to cool.

When the layers are completely cool, whip the cream with the 1/4 cup brown sugar and the remaining 1/2 teaspoon vanilla. To assemble, place one layer on a platter, spread with one-third of the whipped cream, and sprinkle with one-third of the chopped walnuts. Repeat with the other two layers. Sift the 1 tablespoon brown sugar over the top, and decorate with the walnut halves. If you like, you can use them to spell out the name of the deceased.

SERVES 10

ODAY, THE BRITISH REFER TO the post-funeral meal as "being buried with ham." Back in Merrie Olde England, ham was a luxury item, customarily served only to royalty. Among the great unwashed of seventeenth- and eighteenth-century England, funeral cakes were more the norm. Funeral cakes were set out during the service, then wrapped up in paper and placed by the door for mourners to take home as they left the church. The wrapping paper was printed with the name of the deceased and, in some cases, with the image of an hourglass, a skull and crossbones, a coffin, and other ominous symbols of the day. The general custom was not to eat the cakes, but to hold onto them as a keepsake of the funeral and the deceased.

It isn't surprising, then, to discover that most mourners looked forward more to the after-funeral *averil,* which sometimes lasted for days. The term *averil* is derived from "heir ale" (meaning "succession ale"), as the feast was intended primarily to welcome the new heir rather than to say goodbye to the departed. As in other cultures, the estates of most Brits of means at that time allocated a considerable amount of money to pay for the *averil,* in the hopes that the partygoers would pray for the deceased early and often, as they say.

However, considering that people used such celebrations as an excuse to throw caution to the wind in the ways of wine, women, song, and food, it is highly unlikely that much praying got done during the *averil,* unless it was to the medieval equivalent of the porcelain god. One documented *averil* featured two separate meat courses followed by two separate fish courses, each of which contained a minimum of ten different dishes.

Prunes were a common food item at Olde English *averils* for the rich and the poor. They were served plain, stewed, and as an ingredient in meat entrées. It is not known if prunes were included to help facilitate the purging that inevitably followed.

Pork Stew with Prunes and Apricots

3 tablespoons all-purpose flour

1/2 teaspoon salt

1/2 teaspoon garlic powder

1/2 teaspoon paprika

1/2 teaspoon freshly ground black pepper

1/2 teaspoon ground cumin

1 1/2 pounds pork tenderloin, cut into 1-inch chunks

2 tablespoons vegetable oil

3 stalks celery, chopped

2 carrots, peeled and sliced into 1/2-inch rounds

1 yellow onion, chopped

1/4 cup chopped fresh parsley

2 cups chicken broth

1 cup pitted prunes, chopped

1 cup dried apricots, chopped

In a shallow dish, mix the flour, 1/4 teaspoon of the salt, the garlic powder, paprika, 1/4 teaspoon of the pepper, and the cumin. Add a few pieces of the meat to the flour mixture and coat lightly. Set aside. Repeat with the remaining meat.

In a heavy skillet, heat 1 tablespoon of the oil over medium heat. Add half of the meat to cover the bottom of the pan and cook until browned, about 5 to 7 minutes. Remove the meat from the skillet and set aside. Heat the remaining tablespoon of the oil in the skillet and repeat with the remainder of the meat.

Decrease the heat to low and add the celery, carrots, onion, and parsley to the skillet. Cook, stirring constantly, until the onion is translucent, about 5 minutes. Add the broth, pork, and the remaining 1/4 teaspoon salt and 1/4 teaspoon pepper. Increase the heat to high and bring the mixture to a boil. Decrease the heat to low, cover, and simmer for 45 minutes, stirring occasionally, until the meat is tender. Add the prunes and apricots and cook for an additional 10 minutes, until the fruits plump slightly.

SERVES 4

PHILIPPINES

IN THE DAYS BEFORE the native Filipino tribe known as the Ilongot were converted to Christianity by missionaries, they had a curious way of dealing with their grief after the death of a loved one. Pre-1970s, the Ilongot were headhunters, and they believed that the only way to achieve peace after their loss was to add a head to their collection by killing a member of an enemy tribe. This may be among the more extreme methods of mourning, but it was effective.

Among non-headhunting Filipinos, a wake that lasts nine nights after the burial is the custom, especially in rural villages. Each night, villagers gather at the home of the deceased's family. They tell stories, pray, and, like mourners in many other cultures, eat and get drunk. A water buffalo is commonly slaughtered and roasted; lacking this, mourners will settle for a few pigs or a calf. After the meal, adults indulge in copious amounts of coconut liquor while the children munch on sweet rice cakes. Singing, storytelling, and games of mah-jongg help pass the nine nights, although, curiously, the family members don't participate in the festivities. Instead, they stay in their bedrooms and continue to mourn while friends and villagers carry on into the wee hours of the night.

A Culinary Epitaph, Take Eight

Beneath this dust

Lies the smouldering crust

Of Eleanor Batchelor Shoven,

Well versed in the arts

Of Pies, puddings and tarts

And the lucrative trade of the oven.

When she'd lived long enough

She made her last puff,

A puff by her husband much praised,

And now she doth lie

And makes a dirt pie

And hopes that her crust

   will be raised.

—Epitaph for Eleanor Batchelor
Shoven, a baker

Sweet Rice Cake

3 cups coconut milk

2 cups sweet rice,
   uncooked

1 teaspoon salt

1 cup brown sugar

3/4 cup coconut cream

2 tablespoons anise
   seeds

Preheat the oven to 350°F. Grease a 9-inch square cake pan.

In a medium saucepan over high heat, bring the coconut milk to a boil. Stir in the sweet rice and salt. Reduce the heat to medium and cook, stirring constantly, until almost all the liquid is gone. Remove from the heat and add 1/4 cup of the brown sugar. Mix thoroughly. Spread the mixture in the greased pan. Blend the coconut cream and the remaining 3/4 cup brown sugar together and spread over the rice mixture. Sprinkle with anise seeds. Bake for 20 to 25 minutes, until the top is golden brown. Remove the pan from the oven and allow to cool completely before cutting the cake into squares.

SERVES 8

POLAND

M Y OWN HERITAGE IS POLISH, but my grandparents—who came over on the boat in the early 1900s—believed, like many immigrants of their time, that in order to assimilate into American life as quickly as possible they had to totally renounce their village ways.

What a shame. But as I research the funeral customs of Polish peasants, now some of the superstitions one grandmother couldn't help but pass along make sense to me.

"Don't bury me over there," she would say, waving at a particularly dark corner of the cemetery. "It floods." No problem, I thought; she just doesn't want to spend eternity in a water-logged casket. Not true. Water in the grave means that the one lying there in death was a chronic drunk in life.

Another superstition: If you comb your hair with a dead person's comb, your hair will fall out. A bit of dirt stirred into a person's drink means he is next on the Grim Reaper's list. And during the thirteen-day period from Christmas Eve through the Epiphany, the table should be set and meals should be served to the dead at the seats where they sat in life. Though my family didn't follow that custom, I now realize that the fermented oatmeal soup that my father always made each December—which forced us to hold our noses with one hand while using the other to eat the made-only-on-Christmas-Eve pierogies—was perhaps intended to keep evil spirits away from our house. The traditional Polish funeral food is *stypa,* a cracked-wheat dish with poppy seeds and honey.

The High Cost of Dying

Buy a pint of liquor for those who dived for him.

Buy a quart of liquor for those who brought him home.

Buy two quarts of wine and one gallon of cider for jury of inquest.

Buy eight gallons and three quarts wine for funeral.

Buy barrel of cider for funeral.

—Typical liquor order to pay people who assisted in the funeral of a man who drowned in eighteenth-century New England

Stypa Lazanki

*1 cup cracked wheat
(bulgur)*
1 teaspoon salt
4 cups water
½ cup poppy seeds
1 cup honey

In a large saucepan, cover the cracked wheat and salt with 2 cups of the water. Bring to a boil. Remove from the heat and let stand for 30 minutes.

Return to the heat and bring to a second boil. Decrease the heat, cover, and simmer until the wheat is tender. Stir in the poppy seeds. Set aside.

In a small saucepan, cook the honey with the remaining 2 cups of water over low heat for 20 minutes. Cool. Add to the wheat–poppy seed mixture and stir well.

SERVES 6

THE PROTESTANT CHURCH has long been famous for its white-bread approach to religion as well as everything else in life. Bland, unexciting, and you always knew what to expect. As one who was steeped in the Protestant church of the 1970s, I dutifully attended services so dull and insipid that the high note of Sunday morning was when I snuck a sip from my father's cup of instant Sanka.

In this country, at least back then, Protestantism was the norm. Due to its ubiquity—even if someone followed another religion, they certainly had friends who were white Anglo-Saxon Protestants, familiarly known as WASPs—not much was written down. An Internet search for Protestant funeral food generated numerous entries about the etiquette of bringing food to the home of the recently deceased during the weeks following the funeral, but nothing came up about specific dishes or recipes. Searching for funeral food under any of the other cultures in *Death Warmed Over* always generated at least a few fruitful places to explore, but when it came to Protestants, zippo.

So I did the next best thing: I asked a few peers about the kind of food they remember being served at funerals. "Baloney and cheese" was the hands-down answer. These were usually slapped onto a piece of Wonder Bread. An adventurous few, determined to throw off the shackles of humdrum conformist Protestantism, turned the expected sandwich ingredients into a variation on egg and chicken salad, though admittedly, looking back today, you'll need a strong stomach to weather what was assuredly the gourmet cuisine of many a Protestant youth.

A man accustomed to American food and American domestic cookery would not starve to death suddenly in Europe, but I think he would gradually waste away, and eventually die.

—MARK TWAIN

Protestant Funeral Sandwiches

1 8-ounce package
   American cheese
   slices
1 pound sliced bologna
6 eggs, hard-cooked,
   cooled, and peeled
½ cup sweet relish
1 cup mayonnaise or
   Miracle Whip
24 slices white bread
   (preferably Wonder
   Bread)

Place the cheese slices, bologna, and eggs in a food processor. Lightly pulse for a second at a time until the mixture is coarsely chopped. Add the relish and mayonnaise and lightly pulse until the condiments are well mixed. Transfer to a large bowl and refrigerate until ready to make sandwiches, or spread about ⅓ to ½ cup of the mixture on 1 slice of white bread. Cover with another slice of bread and serve, or wrap in waxed paper to hand out after the funeral.

MAKES 12 SANDWICHES

I N ROMANIA, as in other Eastern European peasant cultures, superstitions reveal much more about the culture than mere facts do. If a dog howls in the yard, or an owl hoots in a tree close to the house, or a rooster suddenly sounds like a hen, the villagers are sure that death is on the way, and nothing you say can change their minds.

The food served after the howling dog or hooting owl proves to be right also has its ritualistic place, starting shortly after the death is announced. The grieving family starts to prepare foods to accompany the coffin in a procession from the home to the church and graveyard, usually on the third day after death. They prepare a ring-shaped bread called *colaci*—sometimes hundreds of loaves— to feed all of the people in the village. The group is led by a mourner carrying a pom, the branch of a fruit tree hung with fruits and sweets, and a pot of coliva—bulgur cooked with honey, with candy mixed in.

At the cemetery, relatives pass back and forth over the open grave the following items: a loaf of colaci, a black hen, a candle, a crock of water, and a chunk of salt. These are placed nearby as payment for the gravedigger. After the burial, family and villagers return to the house of the deceased for a feast that consists of more colaci and coliva, and the foods from the pom tree.

2 1-ounce packages yeast

2 cups sugar

1 1/2 cups milk, at room temperature

8 cups all-purpose flour

1 vanilla bean, chopped

6 eggs, separated

1 teaspoon salt

1 cup (2 sticks) unsalted butter, melted and cooled

2 tablespoons vegetable oil

1 egg for brushing the loaves

Colaci

In a medium bowl, mix the yeast with 1 teaspoon of the sugar. Add several tablespoons of the milk and a tablespoon of the flour. Mix well. Cover and place in a warm place to rise, at least 1 hour.

In a medium saucepan over high heat, boil the remaining milk and the vanilla. Remove from the heat and let cool to room temperature.

When the milk is cool, mix the egg yolks with the remaining sugar and the salt, then slowly add the milk, stirring continuously. In a separate bowl, whip the egg whites until stiff peaks form. Transfer the risen starter into a large bowl. Pour in the yolk-milk mixture and the remaining flour, stirring constantly. Mix in the beaten egg whites until incorporated.

Turn the dough out onto a floured board and knead until the dough becomes smooth and satiny. Stir together the melted butter and the oil. Make a well in the dough, add the butter-oil mixture, and work in until the dough becomes smooth. If the dough seems too stiff, add a little milk. If the dough seems too soft, add a little flour. Cover with a heavy cloth and set in a warm place to triple in bulk.

When the dough has risen well, grease four 9-inch round cake pans. Pinch off a quarter of the dough and on a floured board, form it into a loaf shaped like a doughnut, then place in a pan. Repeat with the rest of the dough. Cover the pans and let rise in a warm place for 30 minutes or more.

Preheat the oven to 350°F. Beat the remaining egg and brush it over the loaves. Bake for 30 to 40 minutes, until the tops become golden brown. Remove from the pans and place on a rack to cool.

MAKES 4 LOAVES

EVEN IN THE OLD DAYS of the U.S.S.R., there were significant differences in how people in the different regions of the socialist republic treated their dead—official state policy be damned—and a wide variety of rituals were employed. This is still true today, perhaps even more so. When it comes to funerals, the division of labor among the sexes is firmly entrenched, and there's never any question about who does what: the men build the coffin while the women cry and prepare the food.

One of the more intriguing funeral customs among Russian peasants was followed when a man or woman of marriageable age but not yet betrothed died unexpectedly. Before the funeral, the deceased was dressed in what would have been his or her wedding clothes and then buried in them. In peasant culture, wedding dresses and suits were passed down from one generation to the next, regardless of the current fashion sense. But when the next generation died unmarried, the garment, instead of being passed down to a future bride, was buried with the person for whom it had been intended.

I found no record of specific dishes served after these particularly sad funerals, but there's a good chance that the memory of these young people was honored during one of several Russian pagan holidays commonly celebrated to honor dead relatives. One is the second Tuesday after Easter, which is called the Commemoration of the Dead. Another is the Saturday closest to October 26, or Demetrius Saturday. On these days, the memory of the dead was commonly celebrated with grain: during memorial masses held on those days, people brought porridge and pancakes to church. Afterward, they'd set pretzels, bowls of cereal, pancakes, and bread on the graves of their ancestors.

A Culinary Epitaph, Take Nine

HERE LIES POOR BURTON,
HE WAS BOTH HALE AND STOUT;
DEATH LAID HIM ON HIS BITTER BEER,
NOW IN ANOTHER WORLD HE HOPS ABOUT.

—Epitaph for a beer brewer

Russian Pancakes

1 1-ounce package
   yeast
2 cups warm milk
4 cups all-purpose flour
2 eggs
1/2 teaspoon salt
1 1/2 tablespoons sugar
3 tablespoons vegetable
   oil

In a medium bowl, add the yeast to the warm milk and mix well. Add the flour and blend until smooth. Cover the dough with a clean dish towel or plastic wrap and allow the dough to rise in a warm place, about 2 hours. Add the eggs, salt, sugar, and 1 tablespoon of the oil to the dough. Mix well. Set in a warm place, cover, and let rise again, about 1/2 hour.

Grease a griddle and heat. To test if the griddle is properly heated, sprinkle a few drops of water on the surface; if it sizzles, it's ready. Without mixing the dough again, use a wet spoon to place portions of the dough onto the griddle. Cook on both sides until golden brown. Serve immediately with syrup, preserves, honey, or farmer's cheese sprinkled with sugar.

MAKES 24 PANCAKES

SCOTLAND

THE MOST PREVALENT AND HEART-RENDING funeral ritual around has to be the playing of the Scottish bagpipes. Without the mournful sounds of the pipes—along with the requisite bottle of Scotch whiskey—no Scottish funeral can be considered complete.

During a nineteenth-century Scottish funeral, it was customary for the men of a small Highland village to carry the casket to the churchyard on their shoulders. For sustenance, the town or church would supply them with a gallon of rum for their journey. This was after three days of the wake, at which plenty of food and liquor was available, which probably made them giddy and fatalistic at the same time. Then again, a plate of haggis, the national and much-reviled dish of Scotland, probably had something to do with it. In more refined nineteenth-century households, recognition of class distinction was obvious. At a society wake, the upper-crust mourners would receive wine and cake as their refreshment. In contrast, those below them on the social scale would be lucky to receive some whiskey and cheese. In both cases, the food was served by relatives. The widow or widower dressed in black and sat in a back bedroom with the curtains drawn.

According to Bertram S. Puckle, author of the 1926 book *Funeral Customs: Their Origin and Development,* at that time the most popular food for mourners in Scotland, as in Russia, was pancakes. For one thing, they "were considered as especially suitable to the occasion, and when, as was often the case in village communities, fifty or more persons undertook the vigil, it must have been no light matter to provide each with his accustomed share," he writes. But he then adds another, saner reason: "Often one member from every house in the village would take his turn as a matter of right."

In other words, even drunk as a skunk, how could you screw up pancakes? Or, if you did, the others at the wake—which Puckle describes as more of a party than an outright remembrance of the deceased—didn't much care. Some more traditional Scots, while tolerating pancakes at a funeral feast, would be highly offended if a requisite dish of haggis did not appear on the table. The following recipe is altered a bit to make it easier for non-Scots to stomach.

Americanized Haggis

1 pound ground lamb

1/2 pound lamb liver, cut
   into pieces

1/2 cup water

1 small onion, coarsely
   chopped

1 large egg

3/4 teaspoon salt

3/4 teaspoon freshly
   ground black pepper

1/2 teaspoon sugar

1/4 teaspoon ground
   ginger

1/8 teaspoon ground
   cloves

3/4 teaspoon ground
   nutmeg

1 cup old-fashioned
   steel-cut oats

Preheat the oven to 350°F. Grease a 9 by 5-inch loaf pan.

In a food processor with a chopping blade, process together half of the lamb, the lamb liver, water, onion, egg, salt, pepper, sugar, ginger, cloves, and nutmeg until well combined. Add the remaining half of the lamb and the oats. Process until well combined.

Spoon the mixture into the greased pan. Use a knife to even out the top. Bake for 50 minutes. Cool 5 minutes in the pan. Turn out onto a platter and cut into slices.

SERVES 6

SENEGAL

ENEGAL, on the Atlantic Coast of West Africa, is a former colony of France. Combine this with the national religion of Islam, along with some voodoo-like beliefs among the native people, and the result, when it comes to funeral customs and food, is a hodgepodge of different cultures.

In keeping with the Muslim influence, pork and alcohol have no place in Senegalese funeral customs, but kola nuts do. They are usually passed out to mourners after the burial—in accordance with Islam, only men can attend—and before a funeral feast that is served to both women and men.

After the funeral of her husband, a Senegalese widow enters a period of solitary mourning that lasts for four and a half months. During this time, she does everything possible in order to make herself unattractive, including unbraiding her hair. A sister of her late husband is supposed to do the honors, and if the sister-in-law feels that her late brother's marriage was not a happy one, she will not use a gentle touch as she unbraids the widow's hair.

On the eighth day after death, the male mourners read the whole Koran aloud and slaughter a cow or sheep to offer to Allah and to prepare for another funeral feast. The informal national dish of Senegal, however, is chicken couscous; it is often served at funeral feasts, since it can be prepared ahead of time while the important work of sacrificing cattle or sheep is carried out.

½ cup peanut oil

1 3½-pound chicken,
   into pieces

4 yellow onions, chopp

3 bay leaves

1 ¼ teaspoons turmeri

2 chicken bouillon cub

2 carrots, peeled and
   sliced

1 turnip, peeled and cu
   into 1-inch chunks

1 small head green
   cabbage, shredded

1 teaspoon cayenne
   pepper

1 teaspoon salt

4 zucchini, cut into
   ½-inch chunks

1 eggplant, peeled and
   cut into ½-inch
   chunks

1 15-ounce can garban
   beans, drained

¼ cup (½ stick)
   unsalted butter, melt

1 pound instant cousco

5 tablespoons raisins

Senegalese Chicken Couscous

In a large, heavy saucepan, heat the peanut oil over medium heat. Add the chicken and onions and cook until golden, about 15 minutes, turning occasionally. Add the bay leaves, 1 teaspoon of the turmeric, the bouillon, and enough water to barely cover. Decrease the heat and simmer for 20 minutes. Add the carrots and turnips and continue simmering for 15 minutes. Add the cabbage, cayenne, salt, zucchini, and eggplant, and simmer 10 minutes longer, or until all the ingredients are tender. Add the garbanzo beans. If the sauce is too thin, reduce it over high heat, stirring frequently. Set aside and keep warm.

In a medium bowl, stir the remaining 1/4 teaspoon of turmeric into the melted butter. Add the couscous and raisins and mix well.

Line a couscous steamer (or a colander that will fit into a large Dutch oven) with a dry cloth. Add the couscous mixture and place the colander over boiling water in the Dutch oven to steam the couscous. Cover and cook for about 15 minutes. Serve with the chicken and vegetables.

SERVES 6

SIBERIA
(KHANT)

ALTHOUGH SIBERIA is most popularly known as the region of the former Soviet Union to which citizens who had fallen into disfavor with governmental authorities were banished—much like Bogeyland in *March of the Wooden Soldiers*—Siberia actually has numerous native tribes. Of course, the question comes up: if they were banished, where would they go? In any case, the Khant tribe of Siberia lubricates its funeral services with plenty of alcohol. After a tribal member dies, a wake is held in the deceased's home that lasts for two nights. The next day, the body is prepared for burial, placed in a crude wooden coffin, and transported to the cemetery. As male villagers dig the grave, mourners arrive, build a fire and set a kettle on to boil, and set up a buffet table at the graveside; a typical menu includes bread, dried fish, and candy.

Halfway through the digging of the grave, the men take a break for a bite to eat and a swig of vodka from a communal cup. They finish digging and start to build a small shelter called a gravehouse, complete with roof, over the graveside table. The women place several items of clothing on top of the closed coffin before it is lowered into the grave and covered with dirt. Before the mourners depart, they set a bottle of vodka and some cookies and bread on the table in the gravehouse and knock three times on the shelter door before leaving the cemetery.

Drink Up!

MY GLASS IS RUM.

This epitaph was a stonecutter's mistake—the correct phrase is "My glass is run"—but it probably offers a more accurate appraisal of the cause of the demise of James Ewins, laid to rest in Forest Hill Cemetery in East Derry, New Hampshire, in 1781.

The mourners return after the burial, four days later if the deceased is a woman, and five days later for a man. Except for the burial, the rituals are similar to those of the first day: someone builds a fire, food is laid out on the table, and everybody eats and drinks vodka. Before leaving, they again leave food and drink on the table and knock three times to say goodbye. The gathering is repeated once more, after forty days for a woman and fifty days for a man.

Siberian Cabbage Soup

1 1½-pound portion chuck roast, cut into 1-inch cubes

1 16-ounce can chopped tomatoes

1 large yellow onion, chopped

1 bay leaf

1 clove garlic, minced

3 quarts cold water

1 head cabbage, shredded

2 tablespoons sugar

2 tablespoons white vinegar

Salt and freshly ground black pepper

1 tablespoon freshly squeezed lemon juice

1 pint (2 cups) sour cream

Put the beef, tomatoes, onion, bay leaf, and garlic in a large stockpot and cover with the cold water. Let stand for 1 hour. Transfer to the stove and simmer over low heat, covered, for 2 hours, or until the beef is tender.

Remove the bay leaf and add the cabbage, sugar, and vinegar, and salt and pepper to taste. Simmer for 15 minutes, or until the cabbage is tender.

Just before serving, add the lemon juice and garnish each serving with a dollop of the sour cream.

SERVES 8

SOUTH AFRICA

ALTHOUGH SOUTH AFRICA has undergone many changes in the years since the end of apartheid, funeral customs have remained relatively stable, with white and black people in the cities following rituals according to the Church of England or the Catholic church, and to the Afrikaaner culture, which has a strong Dutch element. The funeral service and burial are pretty much Westernized, for the most part, and offered through a funeral home.

Where things get interesting is among the rural tribes, like the Xhosa in the Transkei and Ciskei regions, for whom the primary religion is ancestor worship through a form of voodoo and witchcraft. According to tradition, only married women are allowed to prepare a dead body for the funeral and burial. They wash and wrap the body in the home of the deceased before handing it to male villagers waiting outside the door of the home. With this ritual, handing the body over symbolizes a child being born; the deceased is being born, too, only into an entirely different world.

> ## A Backyard Buffet
>
> The composer Richard Wagner planned to be buried in a grave in his backyard garden. Frequently, during dinner parties, he would tell guests of his plans mid-meal and escort them to the garden so they could personally view his future home. Afterward, he would enjoy watching to see which of his guests had lost the appetite to finish their meal.

Among the Xhosa tribe, death is regarded as unclean, so most of the funeral rituals involve purifying the surviving family as well as the deathbed. After cleanliness is restored, the spirit of the deceased is allowed to join the ancestors and help assume the task of watching over the living.

One of the oldest rice dishes in South Africa is *begrafnisrys,* or funeral rice.

Funeral Rice

1 tablespoon sugar

½ teaspoon turmeric

1 tablespoon salt

*2 tablespoons unsalted
  butter*

1 cinnamon stick

*1 1-inch strip lemon
  peel*

*2 cups uncooked
  white rice*

1 cup raisins

In a large pot, bring 6 cups of water to a boil. Add the sugar, turmeric, salt, butter, cinnamon stick, and lemon peel. Stir until the sugar is dissolved. Decrease the heat, add the rice, and cover. Simmer for 10 minutes, then stir in the raisins. Cover and cook for an additional 10 minutes, or until the rice is cooked. Remove the cinnamon stick and lemon peel before serving.

SERVES 6

Because spain is a predominantly Catholic country, its funeral services predictably follow the rituals of the religion, albeit with some regional customs stirred into the pot. Up through the 1940s, funeral homes were privately run. After that, the Spanish government got involved in the industry, opening up mortuaries run by local municipalities that were in direct competition with the private homes. When you look at the numbers—in Madrid during the 1960s, the sole privately run funeral home, Pompas Funebres (Funeral Pomp), handled more than 150,000 funerals in an average year—it's obvious why the Spanish federal government decided to jump in.

Pompas Funebres kept an automotive fleet of fifty hearses and fifty limousines to deal with the volume of services. However, one hearse deserves special mention. A horse-drawn hearse from the 1880s was dismantled when motorized vehicles came along, but the body was subsequently set on top of a car chassis, for the family who wanted something to remind them of the good old days.

However, there's another tradition, a pseudo-funeral service of sorts, held each year in many cities throughout the country to celebrate Ash Wednesday and the beginning of Lent. It's also the end of Carnival—the Spanish version of Mardi Gras—and in keeping with the somber mood, many communities will conduct a funeral service called *entierro de la sardine* (burial of the sardine). Though it's not officially sanctioned by the Church, those who march in the funeral procession dress like priests and nuns and conduct themselves in a suitably mournful fashion as they move through the town and on to the cemetery. One of the lead marchers holds up a huge piñata of a sardine. When they reach the cemetery, they bury the sardine. Later, the "mourners" dine on a meal of sardines to mark the end of frivolity, at least for a little while.

Lemons Stuffed with Sardines

6 lemons

1 1/2 tablespoons
  unsalted butter

1 6-ounce tin sardines,
  drained and chopped,
  oil reserved

1 small onion, chopped

1 1-inch strip green bell
  pepper, chopped

1 rib celery, chopped

1/3 cup mayonnaise,
  plus 2 tablespoons for
  garnish

1 hard-cooked egg,
  peeled and chopped

6 sprigs parsley

Melba toast

Cut the tops off the lemons and scoop out the pulp. Cut a thin slice off the bottom of each so it can stand on a plate. Set aside.

Put the butter and reserved sardine oil in a medium saucepan. Over medium heat, stir until the butter is melted. Add the onion and green pepper and cook until the onion is translucent. Transfer from the heat and let cool.

Add the celery, mayonnaise, chopped sardines, and hard-cooked egg and mix well. Spoon into the lemon shells, and place a dollop of mayonnaise on top of each. Place a sprig of parsley on top and refrigerate for two hours. Serve with melba toast.

SERVES 6

SRI LANKA

THE FUNERAL PRACTICES IN COUNTRIES that were once colonies of other nations often reflect the influence of a variety of cultures, given their occupation through the years. Sri Lanka is one such place. The majority of Sri Lankans are practicing Buddhists, but since the country once served as a colony of Portugal, Portuguese rituals show up in the funeral rites as well. A Portuguese-influenced funeral custom among Sri Lankans is to turn all photographs in the house either upside down or backward to face the wall.

> At Irish wakes, mourners were expected to carry salt in their pockets, from which they ate from time to time. The use of salt may be thought in the circumstances to have been merely an encouragement to drink the liquors generously provided, but we find it constantly used for strictly ceremonial purposes in funeral rites.
>
> —BERTRAM S. PUCKLE

Sri Lankans consider death to be unclean, so when a family member dies in the house, relatives believe that the spirit is unclean by association and remains in the house for three months. During that time, any food prepared in the home would be sullied by the spirit, so all food is brought from outside to the family of the deceased.

The funeral and burial are usually scheduled for the day after death, unless it would fall on a Tuesday or Wednesday, which Sri Lankans regard as ill-fated days; in that case, they usually wait until Thursday. However, if the funeral and burial cannot be delayed, the mourners set an egg in the casket with the body; this is supposed to help cleanse the house.

Cremation is the most common method of remains disposal in Sri Lanka. After the body is cremated and the family returns home, the family burns incense or herbs in every room of the house to help hasten the removal of evil from the rooms.

Sri Lankan Omelet

3 eggs

1 small yellow onion, chopped

1 red or green chile pepper, seeded and chopped

2 sprigs curry plant, chopped

2 teaspoons all-purpose flour

1 teaspoon salt

1 teaspoon freshly ground black pepper

1 tablespoon corn oil

In a small bowl, beat the eggs. Add the onion, chile pepper, and curry sprigs to the eggs and stir. Add the flour, salt, and pepper. Mix well.

In a large omelet pan, heat the oil for about a minute over medium-high heat. Pour in half the omelet mixture. Cook for a couple of minutes, then carefully turn over and cook the other side. Transfer to a serving plate and make a second omelet with the remaining mixture.

SERVES 2

I N SWEDEN, a country where over 50 percent of the landmass is covered by forest, the pine tree is an important part of most funeral ceremonies. For one, embalming is referred to as *balsamering*. (No mention is made of whether pine sap is used in place of the usual embalming fluids.) When burial is chosen over cremation, the casket is made of pine. In addition, in rural parts of the country, pine boughs are immediately laid on the ground outside the home when someone inside dies.

When a wife loses her husband, the widow immediately puts on a traditional black hat with a short veil in front to cover the face and a long veil in the back that goes all the way down to the bottom of her coat. The hats of other women who knew the deceased follow other dictates. A daughter's hat doesn't have a veil; instead, a white ribbon is draped around the brim. Other female relatives wear a white collar and apron. Men, regardless of their relationship to the deceased, opt to wear a black suit with a white tie. The entire village also becomes involved in the death of a neighbor by lowering all flags in the neighborhood to half-mast.

Subliminal Messages

Until the early 1800s in Hawaii, most banana varieties were *kapu,* forbidden for women of Hawaii to eat, under penalty of death.

The funeral feast, held either immediately after the burial or several weeks after cremation, is a solemn affair. The family serves a simple meal, and sometimes only something to drink. One source declares that, unlike funeral feasts in other countries—which can get downright bawdy—in Sweden, post-funeral socializing focuses primarily on the dead, with everyone offering multiple toasts to the memory of the deceased.

Funeral Glogg

2 quarts dry red wine

2 quarts muscatel

1 pint sweet vermouth

2 tablespoons angos-
   tura bitters

2 cups raisins

Grated peel of one
   orange

12 cardamom pods,
   crushed

10 whole cloves

1 two-inch piece of fresh
   ginger, peeled

1 cinnamon stick

1 1/2 cups aquavit

1 1/2 cups sugar

2 cups blanched slivered
   almonds

In a large pot, combine the wine, muscatel, vermouth, bitters, raisins, orange peel, cardamom, cloves, ginger, and cinnamon. Cover and let stand at room temperature for at least 12 hours.

Just before serving, add the aquavit and sugar. Place over high heat, stir, and bring to a boil. Remove from the heat, add the almonds, and serve.

SERVES 25

FUNERAL RITES IN SWITZERLAND are usually a simple matter. Manufacturers of elaborate burial clothes and quilted satin casket liners would not thrive in this land, where the body of a deceased man, woman, or child is dressed in a simple white shirt edged with lace and placed in a plain wooden coffin—the six-sided kind, not the rectangular type— lined with a white cotton sheet. Cremation is the norm in this country, which can typically negate the need for elaborate wakes and funeral services.

Little is said about out-of-the-ordinary funeral food customs of the Swiss, and it's assumed that a powdered-sugar-topped sweet pastry like *stollen* wouldn't be served at a Swiss funeral feast, because such food is so closely associated with the cheer of the Christmas season, not the mournful occasion of a funeral—that is, unless the deceased specifically requested it. However, the Swiss did have a peculiar funeral ritual in the late 1800s that involved lemons and the hats of male mourners.

> **Dieting:** A system of starving yourself to death so you can live a little longer.
> —JAN MURRAY

After taking his hat off as a symbol of respect for the dead, a man attending a funeral service was expected to carry his hat under his left arm; no significance is attributed to the left versus the right, but many cultures today still regard the left hand as unclean. Each man would spread a handkerchief in the middle of his hat, place a lemon on the cloth, then roll it up and tuck it inside the hat to secure it under his arm during the procession to the cemetery. Upon arrival, each man would remove the lemon from hat and handkerchief, place it in the grave upon the coffin, and presumably wear the hat for the trip home. Some sources point to the lemon as a symbol of the survivors' grief, but since citrus fruits were rare treats in most northern climes at that time, perhaps it was a way to send the dead off with what amounted to riches. Whatever the origin of the Swiss lemon-in-a-hat custom, the following recipe contains the grief of a lemon along with some sweetness to help cheer up the mourners.

Swiss Lemon Sugar Cookies

½ cup (1 stick)
   unsalted butter,
   slightly softened
⅔ cup granulated
   sugar, plus more for
   sprinkling
1 large egg
Grated zest of 1 large
   lemon
1¾ cups all-purpose
   flour
1 egg yolk beaten with
   1 tablespoon water

Grease several baking sheets and set aside. With an electric mixer at medium speed or by hand, beat the butter in a large mixing bowl until light and fluffy.

Add the sugar and beat until smooth. Add the egg and lemon zest. With the mixer on low speed, beat in the flour until just blended.

Turn the dough onto a floured board and divide it in half. Place one portion between large sheets of waxed paper. Use a rolling pin to roll out the dough to ¼ inch thick. Don't remove the paper. Repeat with the other portion, using new sheets of waxed paper. Refrigerate for about 20 minutes, or until firm.

Preheat the oven to 375°F. Take one portion of dough from the refrigerator and peel the top sheet of waxed paper from the dough. With a 2-inch round cookie cutter, cut out the cookies and place on the prepared cookie sheets, about one inch apart. Repeat with the remaining dough.

Brush the tops of the cookies with the egg yolk–water mixture. Lightly sprinkle the sugar on top of the cookies. Bake for 8 minutes, or until golden. Cool on the sheets for two minutes, then transfer to wire racks and cool completely.

MAKES 50 COOKIES

THAILAND

THAILAND IS A TRADITIONALLY Buddhist country, but some of the religion's mourning rituals are carried out in ways that differ from those of Buddhists in other countries. The wake lasts seven days and is held in a normal fashion: the body is prepared, dressed, and laid out in the parlor of the family home. On the first six nights, Buddhist monks come to the house to say prayers; friends and relatives come too, to visit with the family. Food and drink are served, but unlike at most Western funeral services, in Thailand guests often chat among themselves during the prayers. In addition, at the end of each evening, the family gives food to the monks to take with them.

On the seventh day, the monks escort the casket to the temple, where they conduct a funeral service. As before, people talk among themselves or pray with the monks during the ceremony.

Cremation is the preferred way to dispose of the body, since Buddhists believe that reducing it to ashes is the only way the soul can be freed from the body after death. After the cremation, done right there in the temple, the mourners remain, and they may sit down to a funeral feast in the temple or back at the home of the deceased.

I have a vision of Thai mourners—much like the Lutherans and Mormons who dutifully bring cold salads to a bereaved family's home in the United States—presenting a bowl of Thai Coleslaw to the monks each evening as they head out the door and back to the monastery.

> There was a lamentable amount of ale and whiskey drinking before and after the funeral. If the deceased was a farmer, each of the guests was offered a glass of whiskey at the gate of the farmyard and another on crossing the threshold. On entering the guestroom, a portion of shortbread and another glass of whiskey were handed to him. The religious service was followed by cheese, oatcake and whiskey, and afterwards shortbread and more whiskey. Then the coffin was carried out, followed by all those who were sufficiently sober to walk straight.
>
> W. M. ANDREWS, *BYGONE CHURCH LIFE IN SCOTLAND*

Thai Coleslaw

1 head green cabbage,
*   shredded*
1/2 head red cabbage,
*   shredded*
4 green onions, sliced
1 jalapeño pepper,
*   seeded and diced*
1/4 cup chopped fresh
*   cilantro*
1 cucumber, peeled, seeded,
*   and chopped*
1 red bell pepper, chopped
1/2 cup peanuts, chopped
1/2 cup peanut oil
1/4 cup rice wine vinegar
1/2 teaspoon curry powder
2 tablespoons sugar
2 cloves garlic, crushed

In a large bowl, combine the cabbage, onions, jalapeño, cilantro, cucumber, red pepper, and peanuts. In a smaller bowl, combine the oil, vinegar, curry powder, sugar, and garlic. Add the dressing to the vegetables and toss thoroughly.

SERVES 12

BUDDHISM IS THE PREDOMINANT RELIGION in Tibet; however, the preferred way to dispose of a dead body—cremation—is largely impossible due to the lack of trees for fuel in a country that is mostly above the tree line. And yak dung, while commonly used for cooking fuel, doesn't burn hot enough to totally incinerate a body.

Immediately upon the moment of death, the local lama performs the Passing Ceremony, in which he yanks a hair from the head of the deceased. This allows the soul a means to escape from the body. If the lama is not present at the exact time of death, the family members cover the corpse with a white cloth to keep the soul from fleeing through another orifice before he arrives. If, however, a lama is not handy, a distant lama can carry out the task remotely. No one says what is yanked if the deceased is bald.

After the lama verifies the soul's departure, the body is hacked into pieces and pulverized in a giant mortar and pestle in order to smash up the bones as well. This is to make a nice mixable base for the butter, flour, eggs, and herbs that will be stirred into it, to prepare for what Tibetans call "air burial."

After a Tibetan dies, having a vulture pick the meat from the bones is supposed to increase the amount of good karma the deceased receives in the afterlife; the more appealing the remains are to the birds, the better. In fact, construction on a railroad line connecting Tibet with China in the town of Zhamu comes to a complete halt each time a traditional funeral occurs, since the vultures, being creatures of habit, arrive at the same trackside dive to dine each day.

In contrast to the funeral feasts of many other cultures, Tibetan mourners don't partake in any elaborate dishes. They visit a few days after the deceased has become bird food, and the surviving family serves them rice with vegetables, and beer.

Tibetan Sweet People Cookies

2 1/4 cups all-purpose
   flour

1 teaspoon baking soda

1 teaspoon salt

1 cup (2 sticks)
   unsalted butter,
   softened

3/4 cup granulated sugar

3/4 cup firmly packed
   brown sugar

1 teaspoon vanilla
   extract

2 eggs

1 1/2 cups chocolate-
   covered gummy people
   or coarsely broken
   Teddy Grahams

1 cup chopped nuts (use
   if the deceased was
   male)

Preheat the oven to 375°F. In a small bowl, combine the flour, baking soda, and salt; set aside.

In a large bowl, cream the butter, sugar, brown sugar, and vanilla together. Beat until creamy. Add the eggs and beat thoroughly.

Add the flour mixture and mix thoroughly. Stir in the chocolate "body parts" and the nuts. Drop by rounded teaspoonfuls onto ungreased cookie sheets.

Bake 9 to 11 minutes. Remove to a wire rack and cool completely.

MAKES 48 COOKIES

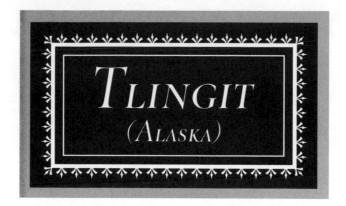

TLINGIT
(ALASKA)

Y OU WOULD THINK IN A PLACE like Alaska, when a member of your tribe dies, you'd just toss them out the door and within a few hours the body would be totally covered in ice and snow, or dragged away by a hungry polar bear.

Not so among the Tlingit tribe in Alaska, a group with as many death rituals and beliefs as those in the more temperate climates. You think *your* in-laws are bad? Tlingit relatives regularly check a widow's face for signs of tears. If they think a widow is inadequately mourning the death of her husband, they can banish her from the tribe because her lack of tears would bring disgrace to them.

The Tlingit also take great pains to make sure not to yawn in the presence of a dead body, because they believe that this makes a very loud noise to the dead and hurts them. They also believe that the animals they eat are regularly reincarnated as people. In fact, they believe that animals are just humans that live under water, like salmon, or in the air, like birds—and that they only assume the appearance of an animal when in the presence of a human. After they're killed for food, they eventually return to their usual habitat and turn into humans again.

The tribe places the death of a tribal member in human form in one of two categories: *wet*, a bad death, and *dry*, a good death. A wet death is cold and damp, and brings shame to the tribe. One example is death by drowning: since the body is often not found, the cycle of reincarnation in the tribe is disrupted. The death of a soldier who was killed in war is considered to be a dry death, with a funeral that brings honor to the dead and the tribe. Instead of being reincarnated within the tribe, they become part of the northern lights, a supreme honor.

Tlingit Fish Soup

2 tablespoons canola oil

1 large yellow onion,
   chopped

2 carrots, peeled and
   chopped

1 head garlic, peeled
   and minced

4 quarts homemade or
   canned chicken broth

1 1/2 cups milk

1/2 cup all-purpose flour

1 pound halibut,
   salmon, or cod, cut
   into chunks

1 10-ounce package
   frozen spinach,
   thawed and squeezed
   dry

Salt and freshly ground
   black pepper

In a large stockpot, heat the oil over medium heat. Sauté the onions and carrot until the onions are translucent. Add the garlic. Cook for five minutes.

Add the broth. Bring to a boil over high heat, then decrease the heat to low and simmer for about 20 minutes.

In a small bowl, mix 1/4 to 1/2 cup of the milk with the flour. Stir until a paste forms. Slowly add the remaining milk to the flour mixture. Stir until smooth.

Add the flour mixture to the broth, stirring constantly. Add the fish and the spinach. Cook until the fish is heated through. Add salt and pepper to taste and ladle into bowls.

SERVES 8 TO 10

TORAJA TRIBE
(INDONESIA)

THE TORAJA TRIBE LIVES on the Indonesian island of Sulawesi, and their funerals are known around the world as exercises in excess and gluttony. The typical funeral has two stages: the first is temporary, primarily consists of mourning, and lasts for only a few days after a death occurs. The body is wrapped and kept in the house until the second stage.

This is the permanent stage, in which the family of the deceased must save up enough money to hold an elaborate ceremony that may continue for as long as a week, with thousands of mourners attending in a village that is specially constructed for the ceremony and burned afterward. The permanent stage can last months, even years—as long as it takes for the family to save the money.

> Recipes without the author, without the cuisine to which they were once a living, seamless part, die.
>
> —JOHN THORNE

When guests first arrive at a Torajan funeral, they give the family of the deceased a buffalo, several pigs, or a bolt of cloth. The family, in turn, gives them some betel nut, cigarettes, and sweet cakes along with whisky and palm wine. Male mourners dress as headhunters and proceed to participate in a number of athletic events, including kickboxing and buffalo hunts. Later in the ceremony, a high Torajan priest sacrifices several of the buffalo to appease the spirit of the deceased.

Then it is time to bury the body, which may have remained in the house for several years or more. The Torajans use a communal tomb carved into the side of a mountain.

Torajan buffalo recipes are few and far between, so instead here is a Torajan barbecue sauce that works well on anything that shows up at a funeral with hooves, single or cloven.

Torajan Funeral Barbecue Sauce

2/3 cup dark corn syrup

1/4 cup creamy peanut butter

1/4 cup soy sauce

1/4 cup cider vinegar

1 green onion, sliced

1 clove garlic, minced

1 teaspoon minced fresh ginger

1/2 teaspoon crushed dried red pepper

In a small bowl or a mason jar, combine the corn syrup, peanut butter, soy sauce, vinegar, onion, garlic, ginger, and red pepper. Mix thoroughly and refrigerate for at least one hour.

MAKES ABOUT 1 1/2 CUPS

TURKEY IS A PREDOMINANTLY MUSLIM COUNTRY, so when someone dies, the family removes the body to a separate room, first making sure that the feet are always facing Mecca. The big toes are tied to each other, the arms are placed against the sides of the body, and a washing ritual begins, while passages from the Koran are read.

Islam dictates that the body be buried as quickly as possible after death and only during the daytime. Exceptions can be made for relatives traveling from a distance, but generally, if a Turk dies in the afternoon, burial will take place the following morning. The body is taken to the cemetery in a simple wooden coffin, but not always buried in it; sometimes it is buried only in a long white shroud, which is sprinkled with rose water before being placed into the grave.

On the fortieth day after the death, relatives and friends of the deceased hold a ceremony at which they recite the *Mevlut,* the Prophet's nativity hymn. Afterward, depending upon the wealth of the family, they may prepare and serve a full meal to people of the entire village, or they may just pass out the sesame-seed confection halvah and Turkish Delight, a candy traditionally made with rose water.

How Come No One's Made a Disaster Movie about This?

On January 15, 1919, a steel tank holding two million gallons of molasses exploded in Boston, creating an eight-foot molasses tidal wave. It killed twenty-one people, knocked over several buildings, and damaged the overhead train tracks. Fermentation was to blame. A hundred and twenty-five lawsuits were filed against the vat's owner, the United States Industrial Alcohol Company. The trial was the longest in the history of Massachusetts. There were so many lawyers involved that there wasn't enough room in the courthouse to hold them all. More than three thousand witnesses were examined and nearly forty-five thousand pages of testimony and arguments were logged.

Turkish Delight

¾ cup granulated
   sugar
1⅔ cups water
⅛ teaspoon cream of
   tartar
2¼ cups confectioners'
   sugar, plus additional
   for coating
½ cup cornstarch
2 teaspoons almond
   extract
½ cup slivered blanched
   almonds

Lightly grease a 9 by 5-inch loaf pan. Combine the sugar, ⅔ cup of the water, and the cream of tartar in a small heavy saucepan over medium heat. Stir until the sugar is completely dissolved and the mixture comes to a boil.

Using a candy thermometer, cook the sugar mixture without stirring until the syrup reaches 260°F (hard ball stage). Remove from the heat and cover.

In a heavy saucepan, combine the remaining 1 cup of water with 2 cups of the confectioners' sugar and the cornstarch. Over medium heat, stir until the sugar and cornstarch dissolve and the mixture comes to a boil. Immediately add the warm sugar syrup and stir until the mixture is smooth. Over high heat, return the mixture to a boil and cook for 5 minutes, stirring constantly.

Remove from the heat. Add the almond extract and the almonds and stir until thoroughly combined. Spread the mixture into the pan. Let the candy rest at room temperature overnight until firm.

Sprinkle the top of the candy with the remaining ¼ cup confectioners' sugar. Cut the candy into bite-sized pieces and roll each piece in additional confectioners' sugar to keep them from sticking together. Store the pieces in an airtight container.

MAKES ABOUT 1 POUND

I N MANY CULTURES, the death of a celebrity or person whose elevated status is miles above that of the plebeians below is regarded as a special occasion, and usually warrants a state holiday. The African nation of Uganda is no different, especially among members of that country's Baganda tribe.

When a Baganda king or clan chieftain is near death, his many wives gather around him to take a closer look, although occasionally they have gotten too good a look and ended his life prematurely by piling on top of him in the erroneous belief that he was already dead. Perhaps this is a belated vengeance tactic to make up for the tribe's now-outlawed custom of having the king's bodyguards kill all his wives, along with several hundred commoners, to ensure that the deceased would not be lonely in the afterlife.

After a king's death, his bodyguards eviscerate their master and remove the intestines. The guards repeatedly squeeze the intestines until they're completely empty, then wash them in beer, reserving the leftover beer for later. They return the intestines to the body and place a catch basin beneath it. The guards then commence to squeeze the body, sometimes for hours, until they have wrung every possible drop of liquid from it, making sure not to spill a drop.

All of the liquid in the basin is then poured into the beer that was earlier used to rinse the intestines. Cups are dipped into it and passed around to all of the guards and all of the wives, and they go back for seconds until the liquid is gone.

I found no mention of other refreshments that are handed out, so, in honor of the Baganda custom, I developed a suitable recipe.

> Fear of the dead is the origin of almost every funeral custom which has come down to use today. From the pomp of the procession to the laudatory epitaph on the tombstone, to propitiate the acute sensibility of the departed.
>
> —BERTRAM S. PUCKLE

Sausage, Cheese, and Beer Soup

2 quarts water

½ teaspoon freshly ground black pepper

1 pound smoked ham, chopped

12 ounces bulk sausage, crumbled

1 cup (2 sticks) unsalted butter

1½ cups all-purpose flour

2 cups cold milk, plus more if necessary

12 ounces sharp Cheddar cheese, grated

1 12-ounce can beer (optional)

In a large stockpot, bring the water, black pepper, and ham to a boil. Decrease the heat and simmer for one hour. Strain the stock and set the ham aside. Return the stock to the pot, keeping it warm.

In a skillet over medium heat, cook the sausage until browned. Set aside.

In a large heavy saucepan, melt the butter over medium heat. Whisk in the flour. Continue cooking, stirring constantly, for 5 minutes. Slowly add the stock, a cup at a time, whisking until smooth after each addition. Slowly add the milk, stirring constantly. Add the grated cheese, a little at a time, stirring until thick, smooth, and melted. If the soup becomes too thick, thin with additional milk.

Stir in the beer, sausage, and ham. Serve immediately to prevent the cheese from congealing.

SERVES 8

LIKE THOSE IN OTHER ASIAN CULTURES, the Vietnamese believe that a funeral is the most important event in a person's life, and the money spent on the ceremony should reflect this, which is why entire family fortunes are wiped out—or massive debt is assumed—in order to have an honorable funeral.

Food plays a big role in a Vietnamese funeral. To prepare the deceased for the journey, at the wake the mouth is kept open so visitors can drop in grains of rice. A bunch of bananas is set on the corpse's stomach to trick the devil out of devouring the intestines. During the wake, most mourners bring a bowl of rice to place on top of the coffin so that by the end of the wake, there will be so much weight on top of the lid that the devil will not be able to get into the coffin.

Before the family sets out for the graveyard, they set up an altar at home for the soul of the deceased. Bowls of rice, a hard-boiled egg, a cup of tea, and the deceased's favorite foods are placed on the altar and carried in the procession, in front of the coffin and behind the Buddhist monks. Other mourners carry immense tables filled with all kinds of food, including whole pigs, wine, bowls of rice, and cakes and other sweets.

After the burial, the tables are set down at the cemetery gates, and the funeral feast begins. Then on the forty-ninth and one hundredth days after the death, the family gathers to remember the deceased with a special meal.

Pushing Up Daisies

A soldier was visiting the spot where a fallen comrade was buried in a foreign country, for the purpose of placing flowers on his grave. On his way he met a native carrying a food offering to the ancestral tomb. Amused by this superstitious absurdity, he asked him when his ancestor would come up from the tomb, as he would like to see him enjoy his meal. "About the same time as your friend comes up to smell your flowers," was the unexpected rejoinder.

—BERTRAM S. PUCKLE

Bun Ho (Beef with Fine Rice Noodles)

6 ounces rice noodles

1 clove garlic, minced

1 yellow onion, thinly sliced

2 inches of lemongrass root, thinly sliced

1 teaspoon salt

1 teaspoon freshly ground black pepper

4 tablespoons nuoc mam (fish sauce)

Pinch of sugar

1 pound sirloin steak, thinly sliced

2 tablespoons peanut oil

½ cup mung bean sprouts

2 cups salad greens

½ medium cucumber, peeled and finely chopped

1 small bunch mint leaves, chopped

4 tablespoons chopped peanuts

Cook the rice noodles in boiling water for 5 minutes. Drain and set aside.

In a medium bowl, combine the garlic, onion, lemongrass, salt, pepper, half the nuoc mam, and the sugar. Mix well. Add the beef to the sauce and marinate, covered, for half an hour in the refrigerator.

Heat the oil in a large skillet and fry the beef to desired doneness. Place one quarter of the bean sprouts, salad greens, cucumber, and mint into each of 4 individual soup bowls, and top with rice noodles. Add the cooked meat to each bowl. Drizzle the remaining nuoc mam over each bowl, garnish with the peanuts, and serve.

SERVES 4

ZOROASTRIANISM

ZOROASTRIANISM IS AN ANCIENT RELIGION that was started in Persia (now Iran) around 1500 B.C. There are still a handful of followers around, in Iran but primarily in India, where they are known as Parsees. The beliefs that ruled the religion from the start are still the basis of the funeral customs that influence followers today.

Demons are the mainstay of the religion, and eradicating them is an important goal in both death and life. Zoroastrians believe that demons can slyly assume a variety of disguises; around a dead body, the favored costume is that of a fly. To keep them at bay, incense is constantly burned on and around the body, but dogs play an important role as well. A dog usually leads the funeral procession to the cemetery, and mourners throw meat scraps onto the ground for the dogs to eat. This serves two purposes. First, it proves that the person is really dead; Zoroastrians think that if the person were merely unconscious, the dogs wouldn't pursue the food scraps so eagerly. Second, it complies with a phrase in the ancient book of Zoroastrianism, which describes how at death "dog and bird will rend your corpse and your bones will be tumbled on the earth."

Though it is not clear whether dogs still perform the function in Zoroastrian society, vultures still do their job in a stone building known as a "tower of silence." Afterward, the soul travels to the Bridge of Judgment, by one of two routes. One is the Endless Light, where the dead eat "the butter of early spring." The other is the wicked underground; there the dead are allowed to eat only spoiled, inedible food until the resurrection.

Worm Food: Two Takes

It costs me never a stab nor squirm
To tread by chance upon a worm
"Aha, my little dear," I say,
"Your clan will pay me back one day."

—DOROTHY PARKER

The play is the tragedy, "Man."
And its hero, the conqueror, "Worm."

—EDGAR ALLAN POE

Zoroastrian Eggs

2 tablespoons peanut oil

1 teaspoon cumin seeds

1 green chile, finely
   chopped

1 clove garlic, chopped

1 medium yellow onion,
   sliced

3 large russet potatoes,
   peeled and sliced

1 tablespoon chopped
   cilantro

4 eggs

Salt and freshly
   ground black pepper

Heat the oil in a large frying pan over medium heat. Add the cumin seeds and allow them to sizzle. Add the green chile, garlic, and onions. Cook until softened.

Add the potato slices and cook for about 5 minutes. Pour in enough water to barely cover the potatoes. Cover and cook over low heat until the potatoes are tender. Sprinkle in the cilantro, stir, and spread the mixture evenly in the pan.

Make four indentations in the mixture, about $1/2$ inch from the side of the pan. Break an egg into each hollow. Cover, decrease the heat to low, and cook until the eggs are just set. Season with salt and pepper to taste.

SERVES 4

Bibliography

Barley, Nigel. *Grave Matters: A Lively History of Death around the World.* New York: Henry Holt, 1997.

Habenstein, Robert W., and William H.Lamers. *Funeral Customs the World Over.* Milwaukee: Bulfin Printers, 1960.

Matsunami, Kodo. *International Handbook of Funeral Customs.* Westport, Connecticut: Greenwood Press, 1998.

Parkes, Colin Murray. *Death and Bereavement across Cultures.* London: Routledge, 1997.

Puckle, Bertram S. *Funeral Customs: Their Origin and Development.* Detroit: Omnigraphics, 1990.

Turner, Ann Warren. *Houses for the Dead: Burial Customs through the Ages.* New York: David McKay Company, 1976.

Wilkins, Robert. *Death: A History of Man's Obsessions and Fears.* New York: Barnes & Noble Books, 1996.

Index